T0285341

DOLLARS, GOLD, AND BITCOIN

www.amplifypublishinggroup.com

Dollars, Gold, and Bitcoin:
The Fed's Hidden Agenda and How to Profit from It

For more information, please contact:
Amplify Publishing, an imprint of Amplify Publishing Group
620 Herndon Parkway, Suite 220
Herndon, VA 20170
info@amplifypublishing.com

Library of Congress Control Number: 2023916668

CPSIA Code: PRV1123A

Hardcover ISBN-13: 979-8-89138-015-8
Paperback ISBN-13: 979-8-89138-148-3

Printed in the United States

To my wife, Jane

DOLLARS, GOLD, AND BITCOIN

THE FED'S HIDDEN AGENDA AND HOW TO PROFIT FROM IT

JOHN S. PENNINGTON JR.

with contributions from

JOHN S. PENNINGTON VI AND **BRIDGER O. PENNINGTON**

an imprint of Amplify Publishing Group

Contents

PART ONE
Boxing In Bitcoin

1. The Number One Product   3
2. Surfing with (Not Against) the Mammoth Manipulators   13
3. Control, Don't Kill   27
4. Reinventing the U.S. Dollar   47
5. The Commerce Clause   63

PART TWO
Blue Jeans to Billions

6. One Man's Trash Is Another Man's Startup   77
7. Negotiation   99
8. Team of Success   123

PART THREE
Building the Wealth Machine

9. With Real Intent   145
10. Raising Capital for Domination—Size Matters   155
11. Increasing the Probability of Success   177
12. The Perfect Question   207

Final Note   231
Acknowledgments   233
About the Author   235

PART ONE

Boxing In Bitcoin

CHAPTER 1
The Number One Product

Americans have an insatiable appetite for pancakes—including me. On most Saturday mornings, I take my family down to a local pancake house and wait thirty minutes for a table. Thirty minutes for pancakes?! Really? Hence the saying, "Selling like hotcakes."

However, there is one product that dwarfs hotcakes—and iPhones and even clothes of any kind—in its popularity. It is almost infinitely better than any product ever invented—the true GOAT (Greatest of All Time). Consider:

- This product comes off the conveyor belt not by the thousands and not by the billions but by the *trillions*.
- People of every make and model lap up this product, wanting more, more, more—no matter how many come off the assembly line.
- Some will lie, cheat, and steal to obtain this precious item.
- Others will work an honest seventy-hour workweek to get more of it.
- Many sacrifice time with their family, spouses, and loved ones to obtain more of it.

- Some go so far as to risk their lives just to obtain a stack of it.
- No matter how many trillions are produced, humankind loves this man-made product more than any other in world history.

What is this product? The U.S. dollar!

We should stop saying that great products are selling like hot-cakes. Instead, we should start saying great products are selling like *greenbacks*!

Throughout its more than one-hundred-year history, the Fed has overseen many aspects of the American economy—seeking to control inflation, keeping unemployment low and gross domestic product high, etc. But the Fed's number one job is to protect and promote the U.S. dollar and create insatiable demand for this wildly successful product. All other tasks are subservient to creating demand and enforcing its acceptance.

To that end, the American dollar is constantly being positioned and marketed to increase sales by leveraging laws, enforcing rules, and intimidating even the most robust adversaries. U.S. regulatory agencies have worked as a team for decades in at least four key ways to build a fundamental, intrinsic, essential, and insatiable demand:

1. U.S. citizens must pay all taxes in U.S. dollars.
2. Crude oil transactions worldwide have required U.S. dollars. After the United States struck a deal with Saudi Arabia decades ago, world banks were required to keep large quantities of U.S. dollars in their reserves to purchase oil.
3. Bank-to-bank transfers via the Society for Worldwide Interbank Financial Telecommunication (SWIFT) system must use only U.S. dollars.

4. U.S. lenders have flooded the planet with irresistibly low-interest loans. If you grab one, you must repay it in U.S. dollars.

All this creates demand for U.S. dollars. As long as this demand exists, is there really any way for the U.S. government to go bankrupt? No. Because they are the source of U.S. dollars—the currency woven into the most powerful aspects of the global economy. How can you go bankrupt when you create a product everyone needs and wants?

The "Idiot" Waiting Tables

Before becoming a serial entrepreneur and a co-founder of a family of private equity investment funds that has grown to over $28 billion in assets under management, I graduated in 1988 with a bachelor's degree in economics. With that perspective, I continually disagree with my friends who criticize the people at the Fed. They claim they're stupid, ill-informed, or completely out of touch.

I acknowledge the Fed does make mistakes—but are they idiots? For me, the best way to decide this is to judge results. Don't listen to what they say. Focus on their deliverables. In this way, the Fed reminds me of a waiter named Sam who has worked at a very fancy restaurant for years. He constantly reminds everyone that he's really bad at math. And it seems to be true. Each time a customer pays for a meal, Sam will inevitably bring back the wrong change. Sometimes the customer will catch the error; sometimes they won't.

When caught, Sam always apologizes and explains, yet again, that he is really bad at math. To lighten the situation, he always jokes that this is why his accounting career went nowhere and why he's waiting tables instead. It seems to work; both the customers and his fellow waiters seem comfortable with the fact that Sam and math just don't get along.

But hold on. The restaurant conducts an audit of Sam's last one hundred customers. Come to find out, Sam brings back the wrong change in favor of himself 100 percent of the time. *That's odd.* If Sam was truly bad at math, wouldn't it be more likely that the change would favor Sam 50 percent of the time and his customers the other 50 percent of the time?

So, who's the idiot? Sam or all those people who believe Sam is terrible at math?

Results vs. words. Deliverables, not verbal spin.

Apply this reasoning to the Fed. They continually explain their plan, apologize for missed inflation targets, and revise them. Just like Sam, they have an agreed-upon expectation with their customers, the American people, and they regularly fail. They tell the public what they want the public to believe, such as "the current inflation is transitory."

These are all verbal spins, verbal distractions—like a good magician who misdirects the audience's attention, so it seems as though a live bird magically came from his hand. They secretly maneuver for inflation to be about 8 percent but tell the public the target inflation rate is 2 percent, then make excuses when the target is overshot. In the Fed's case, the distraction is bad predictions and over- or understated projections. Like Sam the waiter, they carefully craft messaging designed to misdirect and elicit a desired reaction.

The Fed and Congress are like a married couple, where one spends tons of money and the other has to find a way to pay for it. The Fed seeks to maintain the status of the U.S. dollar as the GOAT of all products, but Congress fights that directive by spending more than exists. Within that perspective, the Fed has done a great job thus far covering for Congress's out-of-control spending. Sometimes Congress forgets the government's number one job is to protect and promote the dollar. Why does Congress sometimes miss its fundamental job description? Because a lot of politicians are "temporary employees," unlike most of the people who run the other parts of the government's monetary policies.

Although I have decades of experience in finance and investing, it is important to note that anyone can understand what is happening here and apply it for their benefit. Read between the lines. Don't listen to what they say, and don't take their carefully crafted messaging at face value. Watch what they *do*.

Since the birth (reset) of the fiat U.S. dollar in 1971, we have experienced huge financial changes about every ten years:

- **1987/1988:** The U.S. stock market crash and the fall of the Soviet Union
- **1999/2000:** The dot-com bubble and subsequent stock market crash
- **2008/2009:** The Great Recession and worldwide economic crash
- **2019/2020:** The COVID-19 pandemic and worldwide economic crash

Almost everyone knows about these events. However, not many understand the scope of their significance nor their impact on the world's future probabilities. The fact is these worldwide events transferred vast amounts of wealth to people who have positioned themselves based on what direction the population is headed—where the masses will focus their attention and desires, and—from there—knowing how to fulfill them.

These are "waves" that allow entrepreneurs and others who are thinking strategically (like the Fed) to pounce on opportunities to soar and navigate financial mountains.

Boxing In Bitcoin

The next major wave has been building for the past two decades since the invention of cryptocurrency. The powers behind the greatest product of all time have slowly awakened to the rise of Bitcoin and others as a threat to its dominance. And as they have for more than a century, the Fed found a solution.

I have a theory about what that solution is and how it is being implemented. In the summer of 2020, the U.S. Securities and Exchange Commission (SEC) had just levied a $920 million fine on JPMorgan Chase & Co. (JPMorgan), one of the largest financial institutions in the world. The company had been secretly and illegally manipulating the precious metals markets for almost ten years.* They had manipulated the options and derivatives markets by placing thousands of fake buy and sell orders per day to create a false impression of buy or sell interest, a technique called "spoofing." The reason, said the U.S. securities regulators, was straightforward—huge profits for JPMorgan and its executives.

---

* "JPMorgan Chase & Co. Agrees to Pay $920 Million in Connection with Schemes to Defraud Precious Metals and U.S. Treasuries Markets," U.S. Department of Justice, Office of Public Affairs, September 29, 2020, https://www.justice. gov/opa/pr/jpmorgan-chase-co-agrees-pay-920-million-connection-schemes-defraud-precious-metals-and-us.

Scan the QR code to watch the author explain how JPMorgan was fined almost $1 billion for manipulating the precious metals market.

By that time, I'd acquired a bit of gray hair over the years observing how markets work and are sometimes manipulated. One fact still gnaws at me: though the company did have to pay a nearly $1 billion fine and come clean about how they manipulated the markets, no one from JPMorgan went to jail for fleecing untold amounts of money from the average investor.

With the emergence of Bitcoin as a serious player in the world of global currency, exploding in value from $0.09 per coin in 2010 to more than $20,000 less than ten years later—making it the best-performing asset of any class in the decade—something had to be done.

The Boxing In Bitcoin hypothesis states that the U.S. government, via the Fed and the SEC, extracted the knowledge they needed to manipulate and control the Bitcoin market from their 2020 legal battle with JPMorgan. The combined forces of the Fed, the SEC, and the U.S. government began using this new information in 2021 with a clandestine strategy to control the price of Bitcoin on the open worldwide market—boxing in and seeking to control the fast-growing competitor in a campaign that will likely last decades until the U.S. implements the launch and full adoption of its own United States digital dollar (USDD).

Predicting the future is futile. Understanding probabilities, on the other hand, can greatly boost success. My ongoing theme from here on is: no predictions, just probabilities. Accordingly, I am giving my hypothesis an 85 percent chance of being correct.

Your Number One Product

The idea that the federal government learned how to box in Bitcoin by going after a company for doing precisely the same thing with precious metals may anger you. Yes, it's diabolical. But it's a remarkable critical-thinking exercise as well.

If you're a business owner, an entrepreneur, or just an ordinary investor, try to look past your anger to see a bigger picture and, more importantly, a bigger *opportunity* available for yourself. As we will cover in this book, there's a lot that we can all learn not only from what the U.S. government is doing with Bitcoin but what it has done historically to protect its number one product.

The thought exercise begins with a simple but very important question:

What is your number one product?

The answer is simple and just as important—YOU! The human brain is the most complex object ever discovered in the entire history of the universe. By paying attention to the information streaming past you every day (whether it's the price of Bitcoin, a new business strategy, or a probability of future events), by understanding the planet-changing waves going on around you and implementing the right strategies as the Fed has done with Boxing In Bitcoin, you can turn yourself into a product that everyone needs and wants.

This book is about much more than cryptocurrency, the government, and the history and future of money. I've designed it—using lessons from my own life and career as well as the macroeconomic strategies of the Fed in its battle with Bitcoin, gold, China's yuan, and beyond—to help improve our understanding of the real financial game that is being played out on the worldwide stage and reveal how successful entrepreneurs can and have built immense, sustainable wealth.

For example, part of the U.S. dollar's success is its large volume. You can't print your own currency like the Fed. But you can scale your business. One of the easiest ways to scale is within a business model of a private equity fund, a limited partnership—building your own wealth machine. This type of size allows for the boxing in of your success. Controlling your own outcomes. Sitting in the driver's seat of your life instead of the passenger seat.

For that reason, I've devoted the last four chapters to the dos and don'ts of building such a partnership. It's also why I included my sons—both of whom built their own successful funds in their twenties and thirties and also now teach others how—as contributors to this book, as their stories provided important examples of how a young person's thinking can evolve from "small" to "supersize."

It is my goal for you to finish this book with not only a better understanding of how attainable wealth is but a better understanding of your personal potential to get yourself there—no matter your starting point. Throughout the chapters, you will find NOTE TO SELF boxes, which provide us with helpful reflections on how to inspire change and growth in your own journey. At the conclusion of each section, you'll find a Boxing In Basics section that summarizes the most important lessons from each chapter.

BOXING IN BASICS

1A. I believe the U.S. government learned how to control and manipulate commodities from JPMorgan and leveraged that scheme to control the Bitcoin market to the U.S. dollar's benefit.

1B. The government is doing this because Bitcoin was becoming a threat to America's number one product of all time—the U.S. dollar.

1C. Business owners, entrepreneurs, and others in leadership roles can all learn from what the U.S. government is doing with Bitcoin.

1D. One essential lesson from the Bitcoin situation is to pay attention to what others *do*, not what they say. Don't fight forces or events when you cannot win. Instead, find a surfboard and ride the wave as far as it can take you.

CHAPTER 2

Surfing with (Not Against) the Mammoth Manipulators

When the world changes, there is opportunity.

This is when an entrepreneurial mind kicks into a state of hyper-awareness and hyperfocus—and this focus usually pays dividends. It asks questions like: *What will people do? How will they react? And when the herd starts to move, what waves (also called business opportunities) will they cause?*

If we're not intentional, these major shifts cause us to lose perspective quickly. Depending on their context, they cause anxiety and confusion and make many consider where their lives are headed when they're impacted by major waves of change. However, if you want to take advantage of the opportunities surfacing that many people miss, these inflection points in history should cue you to pay attention and shift your focus outward.

When I was a younger man, I would often fight against such sweeping change. I pushed back because of a principle I had ingrained in my soul (or so I thought). But now as I reflect as an older, more experienced person, I respond differently.

Picture this: I'm standing knee-deep in the ocean with my arms outstretched, trying to stop a wave from coming in and hitting the beach. That's me as a younger man. But now that I have some grey hair, I don't try to stop waves. Instead, I attempt to find the best surfboard I can and ride the wave as far as it will carry me. This practice has served me well in all areas of my life, not just my finances. Don't fight the Fed. Discover what they are doing and go with it.

That's one of the most important lessons Boxing In Bitcoin can offer us: **Rather than fight a powerful tide, learn to leverage it.** As I pointed out earlier, Bitcoin is anything but the government's first foray into stacking the deck in its favor. It is far better to ride it as far as it can take you than to get washed away trying to stop it.

One example of sweeping change like this took place about eighty years ago.

Bretton Woods

In July 1944, more than 1,000 people from forty-four countries met in Bretton Woods, New Hampshire, for the United Nations Monetary and Financial Conference. Their task: To reset world currency prices. The result of this meeting became known as the Bretton Woods Agreement.

By this time, the Allies knew they were going to win World War II. Accordingly, leaders throughout the world decided they needed to rearrange how varied currencies would interact with one another. At the conference, they decided that gold bullion would back the U.S. dollar, and, in turn, the dollar would back other world currencies. For instance, after 1944, the French franc and other currencies were not backed by gold but backed by the U.S. dollar—which was backed by gold.

This reset carried sweeping consequences, especially for the United States. In particular, the arrangement inherently caused the majority of all oil transactions throughout the world to be executed in U.S. dollars, as I touched on in chapter 1. Naturally enough, this created huge demand for every country to own and maintain a reserve of U.S. dollars. If anyone wanted to purchase a tanker of oil, the dollar was the only game in town as a medium of exchange.

Here's how that might play out. If in the year 1974 a German buyer wanted to purchase a tanker of oil from Saudi Arabia, they could not simply wire Deutsche marks to Saudi Arabia. Instead, they had to wire their Germany currency to the New York Federal Reserve using the SWIFT system, convert the marks into U.S. dollars, and then wire those dollars to the Saudi Arabia suppliers.

Complicated by design, it was also a pure windfall for the United States. Since everyone else needed dollars to buy oil, demand for the U.S. currency exploded. And, as a result, the U.S. government kept printing more and more.

But there was even more manipulation to come.

> NOTE TO SELF
> **Position for Power**
>
> To have a supersized company, follow the U.S. dollar's example by positioning your number one product exactly in the crossroads of customers.

Manufacturing Monopoly

True to the expectation of Bretton Woods, the Allies did win World War II about one year later. And, in addition to the rearrangement of the dollar's relationship to other currencies, other circumstances also played in the United States's favor.

After the war, the United States became the world's superpower, primarily because it had more than 60 percent of the world's gold reserves, nuclear capabilities, and—no less important—functioning manufacturing facilities. I have heard economist "experts" at my barber shop or on social media pining for the 1950s when a family could have a stay-at-home spouse, several children, a house in the suburbs with two tail-finned Chevys in the garage, and extra cash every month to save for retirement.

Unfortunately, that's a lovely picture that—once again—relied on a stacked deck. This kind of idyllic prosperity was made possible for some because, post–World War II, the United States had almost zero competition for manufactured products. Factories in Germany, England, France, Japan, Russia, Italy, and China had been destroyed or severely damaged in the war. Outside the United States, most of the industrial world was out of commission. If someone wanted to purchase an automobile, they had to get it from the U.S.A. It was a monopoly that *supercharged* the economy, and it helped build an enduring picture of the idealized American life many would work toward for decades after.

But not only did the rest of the world eventually catch up, they also caught up with better products than Americans were manufacturing. However prosperous the manufacturing monopoly might have been, for a few decades it fostered an arrogance—an uppity American attitude that people around the world would purchase anything American made, even if the quality was substandard. Detroit pumped out mediocre or worse cars—hello, Ford Edsel!—and buyers throughout the world had to settle for them because there was no alternative. Detroit has since corrected this and can compete with any automobile manufacturer worldwide.

But manufacturing wasn't the only market the United States cornered. After the end of WWII, almost all naval forces around the world were decimated except for the United Kingdom and the United States. A navy is one of the most expensive operations for a country to own and operate, let alone replenish after resources are depleted in one of the worst conflicts in world history. So, after the war, the United States essentially offered to deploy its navy to protect other countries' shipping lanes of commerce. Don't worry about Blackbeard and other seagoing cutthroats, the naval forces of the U.S. Navy would have your back. And all we asked was that these countries transact their oil purchases in U.S. dollars. It seemed like a fair trade—"free" naval protection for using the U.S. dollar for oil supplies. A move that helped boost the American dollar into the number one product of all time.

And the deal pretty much held up. We know of two people who tried to transact large quantities of oil without using U.S. greenbacks. One was Saddam Hussein—president of Iraq—who met his demise just a few years later via a roundabout maneuver from the U.S. government. The other was Muammar Gaddafi—dictator of Libya—who also was deposed and killed shortly after the U.S. distanced itself from his regime.

In February 2022, Russia invaded Ukraine. In response, U.S. President Joseph Biden cut off Russia's ability to use the SWIFT system and seized American-dollar bank accounts of Russian oligarchs. When Russian President Vladimir Putin announced that all Russian oil sales would be transacted in gold or the Russian ruble, Biden responded by stating Putin "cannot remain in power." Supporting a change in leadership is very different from denouncing the Russian invasion of Ukraine. Moreover, it is interesting that President Biden only called for this after Russia's refusal to use

U.S. dollars for oil transactions, not after Putin authorized human rights violations and the murdering of innocent civilians.

What happened next? Russia's two huge underwater natural gas pipelines (Nord Stream I and Nord Stream II) were destroyed by someone with access to a deep underwater submarine. Coincidence?

The moral of the story: the world's superpower has a product that you better not mess with.

A Reset of the U.S. Dollar Is Not So Golden

After the stock market crash of 1929, the SEC was formed to control illicit raising of capital and stock market abuses. Several of its landmark actions came in 1933 and 1934. Working in concert with the U.S. Treasury Department, the Fed, and President Franklin D. Roosevelt, the Gold Reserve Act of 1934 made it illegal for any U.S. citizen to own gold bullion. Owning a gold necklace or gold watch was permitted, as was owning collector coins, but owning more than three gold coins or gold bars was against the law. My grandparents or your grandparents could have gone to jail for as long as ten years if they were caught with a mere four gold coins in their pocket. Instead, they were bound by law to sell their gold to the government, which—after surrender—was pegged at the price of $35 an ounce, to be stored primarily at Fort Knox.

The new gold laws had no effect on other countries. Nations such as France and Great Britain could still exchange their U.S. dollars for gold bullion. The printing of paper money ballooned in the United States. This came to a head in 1971 when countries such as France started to redeem their U.S. dollars for gold bullion in massive quantities.

In response, U.S. President Richard Nixon discontinued the gold standard (backing the dollar with gold). Although it was labeled "temporary" at the time, it effectively ended a longstanding relationship between gold and the value of money. Over time, an ounce of gold came to be worth roughly 12 ounces of silver, primarily because for every 12 ounces of silver mined, 1 ounce of gold was mined. Hence the ratio.*

Just like that, gold was a thing of the past, not needed—paving the way for the third reset (1933, 1944, 1971) of the U.S. dollar, which was then nicknamed "petrodollar" for obvious oily reasons. After the change in 1971, the U.S. dollar became theoretically backed by the ability of the U.S. government to collect tax revenue. This is known as a "fiat" currency, meaning a form of exchanging value from one person to another. Basically, if workers use their skill set to produce goods or services, the government would take a portion in the form of a tax, thus transferring value from the goods or services to the government itself.

Scan the QR code to watch a newscast of President Nixon removing the U.S. dollar from the gold standard on August 15, 1971.

---

* That ratio does not hold true today, as silver is $20 to $25 an ounce and gold is $1,800 to $2,000 an ounce.

But there is a central, inherent risk to every type of fiat currency. Inevitably, over time, the value of fiat money goes to zero. Why? Because a government cannot resist printing more fiat currency when it overspends. All governments in history with fiat currency have eventually overspent. The reason, simply enough, is that nothing of tangible value is supporting it. With gold or silver, that's not the case—currency is backed by a physical substance with an established (albeit fluctuating) value. But, unto itself, paper money's core value boils down to the paper on which it's printed as well as the massive military that forces its worldwide adoption. Bitcoin has no military; therefore, it will take much more time for worldwide adoption.

Printing of fiat currency, in some cases, can lead to hyperinflation that's almost unimaginable. The formula is simple: Keep printing more and more paper money, and the cost of buying almost anything shoots through the roof. Zimbabwe tried this, snowballing to the point of printing a single piece of paper money that read "One Hundred Trillion Dollars"—at one point it was equal to about $7. That meant a lunch out in Zimbabwe would set you back 100,000,000,000,000 ZWD. (Try figuring out the tip for that.)

Weaponizing Interest Rates

The U.S. government does not limit its manipulations to gold, oil, and the like; those are hardly the only armaments they've used to boost the preeminence of the dollar. In December 2018, the Fed announced they would increase interest rates three separate times

NOTE TO SELF
Watch for Ripples
A ripple can become a wave. Pay attention to confusing news. You may uncover a billion-dollar pattern.

in the coming year. Then, less than forty-five days later, they said, "Oops, we made a mistake. We're not going to increase interest rates three times . . . (wait for it) . . . instead, we're going to *cut* them three times."

When I heard this, my economic brain went into overdrive. *Whaaaat just happened?* I knew it was something very big—I just wasn't certain exactly what—but I knew I had to focus and pay close attention. Information was zooming past me, so I kept my economic antennae extended for additional information. Then in March 2019, I read a report that said there were more than $3 trillion worth of negative interest rate bonds trading in Europe. This is a bond that is mathematically guaranteed to lose money. *Why would that even exist?* I asked myself.

Remember, I have a bachelor's degree in economics. I have educational and professional background in the approaches, processes, strategies, and nuances of how we use and interact with money. Over my entire career up to this point, I had never read a book about, read an article about, or ever heard a single mention of a *negative interest rate bond*.

Then, in the summer of 2019, the European negative interest rate market ballooned to more than $14 trillion in value. People, institutions, and fund managers were buying and selling bonds at zero or negative interest rates on a massive scale. Why? To lock in their losses? It made no sense—yet it existed to the tune of $14 trillion!

Some context would be helpful here. In January 2019, the United States was enjoying:

- Record low unemployment rates
- Record low interest rates
- Solid gross domestic product (GDP)
- Low inflation rates

> **NOTE TO SELF**
> ## Lose to Gain
> Think long term. Taking a financial loss on a product for a short period of time to gain strategic market share is a lesson well learned from the greatest product of all time.

In economics, those four things rarely happen at the same time—usually, two or maybe three will happen concurrently, but not all four. So, knowing those positive factors, what was the Fed doing in January 2019 when they said they were reversing their decision and would lower interest rates three times? *They were positioning and manipulating to make sure the world continued to use the U.S. dollar over all other currencies by making it cheap and plentiful.*

Flood the world with cheap dollars that entice everyone to take on debt that must be paid back in those same dollars. If the Germans were going to leverage zero to negative interest rates, the Fed simply lowered interest rates to compete. This strategy was not limited to the short term, either. Massive worldwide debt in U.S. dollars would bolster worldwide demand for dollars for decades to come.

Dangle cheap debt, lend more dollars, and require that this debt be repaid in U.S. dollars. That's rock-solid demand in place for many years to come.

If you need more evidence that the United States will stay the course, consider this: The United States is approximately 256 years old. At least 40 percent of all U.S. dollars currently in existence were created within three consecutive years—2019 to 2022 (including the Eurodollar, the U.S. dollars in Europe). The printing presses have certainly been humming lately.

Can All This Last?

As a team, the U.S. government, including the Fed, the Treasury, the Navy, the Internal Revenue Service (IRS), and the SEC have created the most profitable product the world has ever known. And let's not forget efficient—ink and paper are no longer necessary to produce more dollars, especially Eurodollars. All that's needed now is a computer and a bank. When an entity can manufacture a product by the trillions that people only want more of, then it's clearly addressing the needs of the herd—a principle I cited at the outset of this chapter.

So, that begs the question: Is this situation here to stay?

As you might imagine, other global superpowers China and Russia are not happy that most of the world must purchase crude oil in a currency other than their own. Since the 2008 global financial crisis, they've both increased their physical gold reserve supply each and every year. Why? Because they—possibly—see a future probability: If there ever is a crack in confidence in the U.S. dollar and its world dominance, they can announce to the world: "We have gold backing our currency. And we're going to begin using that currency to purchase oil." As a result, the supply and demand ratio for U.S. dollars would weaken.

China and Russia are strategically maneuvering for this possible event. The question is: Can they pull it off?

They're certainly trying to position themselves from a political standpoint. China has gutted the country's constitution to allow the president a lifetime appointment, should he desire it. Russia's president has been in office for more than two decades and may be there for another two, despite the debacle that has been the invasion of Ukraine. However forced, that's the kind of stability that lends itself to long-term planning.

By contrast, China and Russia see every U.S. president as an elected *temporary* employee—four to eight years at the most. That's a very short time on the world political stage, effectively limiting the president's ability to execute strategies that can be replaced by his or her successor.

Therein lies yet another lesson that Bitcoin, gold, oil, and various other manipulative dances can offer us. As I discussed earlier, don't try to fight opposing forces embedded in strength. Instead, find yourself the best surfboard and ride it as far it will take you. And that's just what the leaders of China and Russia are doing. Not trading punches. But positioning themselves to ride the wave and outwait their opponents.

BOXING IN BASICS

2A. Rather than fighting a powerful tide, learn to leverage it.

2B. The U.S. government has been stacking the deck to protect its number one product—the dollar—for years, starting with the Bretton Woods Conference of 1944.

2C. Since most navies were decimated during World War II, the United States essentially offered to deploy its navy to protect other countries' shipping lanes of commerce. In exchange, participating countries would, as an unwritten rule, transact all oil purchases in U.S. dollars.

2D. To protect the dollar, the Fed has repeatedly tinkered with interest rates.

2E. In summary, pay attention to waves and learn how to catch one. Like the government, there are ways to leverage them to your advantage.

CHAPTER 3
Control, Don't Kill

Which of the following statements are true?

1. The Fed doesn't even care about Bitcoin.
2. The Fed would never try to control Bitcoin.
3. The Fed does not view Bitcoin as a threat to the U.S. dollar.
4. The number one job of the Fed—again—is to protect and promote the U.S. dollar.

The first three statements are absolutely false. The fourth is a certainty.

Price is a language. Price tells us something about *everything*. Every day, economists figure out what message the price of something seeks to convey; they try to understand its significance. But price is not a clear, forthright message; it is simply a clue that can lead us to a better understanding. Price information enables a calculation of probability scenarios. Compare the price of a gallon of root beer to that of a gallon of gasoline at the corner store. What can that tell you about the community you live in? Once studied, these scenarios allow us to place ourselves in the middle of any upcoming wave, ready with the best surfboard we can find for the longest and most rewarding ride possible.

This brings me back to the bizarre example I shared in the prior chapter—that of European bonds paying a negative interest rate. *Why*, I kept wondering over and over, *would anyone buy something that was consciously designed to lose money?* Even someone who has never stepped into an economics class would be as dumfounded as I was.

In my quest to make sense of all this, my Econ 101 antennae picked up on a couple of other examples of things that have gone negative:

- **Negative birth rates.** Countries need to have 2.1 children per woman to sustain current population levels. As it happened, in 2019, more than half of the countries in the world—more than 51 percent—had a negative birth rate (less than 2.1 children per woman). For years, Japan and Germany have had extremely low birth rates—1.36 and 1.6, respectively.* The price (physically and/or financially) of having several children was apparent for city dwellers who began to delay or forego having children. But the expense of having a family wasn't the sole cause of this decline. Even more extreme was China's birth rate, due to the country's long-standing policy of limiting couples to a single child, which led many to undergo abortions to avoid birthing females in favor of males. Not only did this leave the country with 37 million more men than women, but some estimates hold that China's overall population will shrink from 1.4

---

* "Fertility rate, total (births per woman)," The World Bank, revised 2022, https://data.worldbank.org/indicator/SP.DYN.TFRT.IN?end=2021&most_recent_value_desc=false&start=2021&view=chart.

billion to 750 million by 2080—that is literally the entire country's current population cut in half—and, with it, a 50 percent drop in demand for food, oil, housing, and any other necessity you can think of.

- **Negative oil prices.** No one was buying oil in March 2020 because of COVID-19. The reasons were simple: No one was driving to work, no planes were flying, and cruise ships never left their docks. Gasoline was effectively unnecessary. As a result, oil tankers stopped serving as a means of transport and effectively became floating storage units. And if you happened to own oil options in the futures market that you couldn't sell before they expired, you had to take delivery. The problem was, since oil simply wasn't selling, there was no place to store it—every location was full to the brim. Desperate, traders in the futures market tried selling oil down at $20—which is an unheard-of price. No takers. Ten dollars a barrel, then $5—still not a buyer in sight. Then the oil was yours for free, just so they didn't have to take delivery. Crickets. Ultimately, a solution was found. People holding the oil contracts had to *pay* $20 a barrel for someone to take physical delivery of the oil. Oil was going for a negative $20 a barrel; this was completely unprecedented.

Negative Interest Rates—Once More with Feeling

That brings me back to Europe and negative interest rate bonds. Why were they being snapped up like proverbial hotcakes? Here's one viable possibility: Let's say a country in Europe has a state-sponsored pension fund for its working class. Each payday, companies all over the country deduct a few dollars (or marks, francs, Euros, whatever) from each person's payroll check and send them to the sponsored retirement pension plans to fund employees' individual retirement nest eggs. The fund managers in charge of investing these retirement funds have the responsibility to place that money in solid investments, thereby enabling millions of people to retire at age sixty-five.

But there's a problem. This pension fund's charter (investment rules that the fund is bound to follow) is very conservative, limiting its portfolio to low-risk European Union government-guaranteed bonds. And in 2020, the government-guaranteed bonds of the EU countries were trading at zero percent or negative yielding rates.

With no place to deploy the capital in a good investment, the most obvious solution would be to simply stash the cash in a bank account—admittedly, at zero interest return but far better than a negative payout. But yet another wrinkle emerges. As weeks and months pass with no improvement in bond yields, a government auditor notices the mountains of cash piling up and cites another element of the fund's charter—the fund is required to invest that money in some form of government-guaranteed securities. Merely sitting on the cash violated the fund's charter—this approach was not an option. Accordingly, the fund managers must purchase negative yielding government bonds that are guaranteed to lose money, because they are forced to do *something* with the funds being collected.

Let me repeat that: They're *required* to invest in something even when there are no potentially profitable options, so they had to go with an ironclad guarantee of losing money. Because evidently, holding cash is riskier than a negative-yielding government bond.

But, once again, there's manipulation afoot. The true heart of the issue isn't governments making certain fund managers follow stipulated rules. Rather, governments were printing so much fiat currency, purchasing their own bonds, driving up bond prices, and simultaneously reducing yields to below zero levels for the purpose of the super stimulation of their economies. That's the real reason. Forcing administrators to follow the rules so closely even when the rule no longer made sense was a purely self-serving move on the part of the government.

A good way to understand negative interest rates is the sandy beach analogy. Imagine you are sitting on a vast beach. I walk up to you with a handful of sand and ask how much you would pay for it. "Nothing," you reply. "Can't you see? I have a plethora of sand already." However, you tell me you would be happy to store my handful of sand—for a fee. That's what banks in Europe were doing. Since abysmal bond yields were flooding their vaults with a huge wave of cash, the banks got on the zero-interest surfboard and charged fees to hold your cash. Give your cash to the bank and pay them a fee to hold it. Too much sand on the beach—who wants that?

Furthermore, it forced a swift and strong response. The Fed effectively lowered its interest rates to virtually zero to compete against extremely cheap European currency. Even though the Fed's hand was forced, it was no less manipulative than some of the other schemes we've already discussed (remember, to buy crude oil, you need Yankee greenbacks). By flooding the world with loans in U.S. currency that must be paid back in U.S. dollars, the Fed created immense demand for decades to come. With enough product in circulation, the United States could muscle out other countries' cheap currency. If you must borrow money, borrow American.

Relevant to Bitcoin

So, what does all this have to do with Bitcoin, and more significantly, what can the government's efforts against it teach us about running more successful and rewarding businesses and organizations?

> **NOTE TO SELF**
> ### Keep Your Guard Up
> Assume competitors are continually plotting to storm your castle. Thwarting any siege must be part of your risk matrix plan.

When running probabilities for outcomes, the overriding factor for increasing accuracy is the ability to *realistically size up your opponent*. As we all know, every business venture has risk. The inability to understand risk can only lead to problems and outright failure.

Accordingly, great businesspeople know how to identify and reduce risk. Risk can never be completely eliminated, but it can be mitigated once it is properly identified. That's why understanding who or why someone would become an adversary is strategically necessary. In the case of the Fed, as it focused on its European competitors, it recognized that it was necessary to cut interest rates to the bone to maintain the dominance of the U.S. dollar throughout the world. And it's that same almighty dollar that turned its focus in 2021 to become Bitcoin's imposing adversary.

Obviously, Bitcoin has a very large problem (perhaps better phrased as "a very large enemy"). In fact, Bitcoin has a destiny, by definition of its very design, to unfortunately go to battle with the biggest, most powerful opponent in history. From the very nanosecond of its creation, at the inception of the first Bitcoin-mining computer, the epic clash was inevitable. The two forces were on a collision course, and the impact is inevitable.

But there's yet another issue. Unlike gold, which the United States gobbled up from private owners in the 1930s, cryptocurrency can't be confiscated. It isn't tangible. It has no borders. Not only is there worldwide demand, but its independent nature is outside the box of typical world fiat currencies. In some ways, it is the most accessible and transferrable of all currencies in history.

Don't Kill Bitcoin, Just Control It

So, can the Fed crush Bitcoin? Probably not. But there are alternative strategies to overpowering this massive wave.

Bitcoin's strengths are, in a strange way, also its weaknesses. First, since there can only be 21 million Bitcoins in existence, its enemies enjoy a fixed and defined playing field. Bitcoins, in quantity, are ultimately mathematically capped to ensure a virtual currency with absolute scarcity. This offers the Fed a set of unchangeable parameters that can be mathematically manipulated (at least for the short term). Second, Bitcoin has no military and appeals to the retail investor—individuals who buy and sell assets for themselves instead of on behalf of a country—and these are people who we all know can be squeezed and emotionally drained as a result of a fatigued long game. Remember, most battles in history were won by attrition.

Is it possible for the Fed to eliminate Bitcoin? That's not likely. But, then again, that is not the goal, either. The goal is just to control it, not kill it. Cage it, box it, and contain it. Killing it would just give way to the rise of a new alternative cryptocurrency that the Fed would then go after all over again, which would almost be more work on their end. Their approach is to keep it suppressed for decades, cage it, and make sure it never completely dies. Control it until the U.S. digital dollar is launched and adopted. This is the plan of the Fed for the future of Bitcoin. Box in Bitcoin. They are controlling their competition.

Up until November 2021, Bitcoin pretty much acted according to plan. Then something changed. The SEC allowed an exchange traded fund (ETF) for Bitcoin *futures* to enter the market. (An ETF is similar to a mutual fund, employing a pool of resources, but focused on a particular index.) Notice what the SEC did not allow. Citing myriad illogical excuses, they did not permit an ETF that actually *purchases* Bitcoins. But the SEC did allow an ETF for derivative financial contracts that require the purchase or sale of an asset at a predetermined future date and price. In so many words, option prices rarely have anything to do with the real thing but can be used to manipulate its price.

Once more, let's pay attention to actions rather than words. Allowing an ETF that actually purchases Bitcoin would hinder the government's efforts to control Bitcoin. Instead, this SEC maneuver further strengthened the Fed's ability to control Bitcoin. The SEC and Fed were working as a team. Eventually, the SEC will allow a company to launch an ETF that buys and sells actual Bitcoins, but my guess is that such a company will be extremely large and in cahoots with the U.S. government to promote and protect the U.S. dollar. Only then would this ETF be allowed to exist.

And where did the Fed learn this scheme? Why, JPMorgan, of course—the institution we discussed in the first chapter that controlled the precious metals markets for close to a decade by manipulating the futures market of silver. The likeness between these situations is hardly coincidental.

Boxing In Bitcoin Theory

So, given all the cloak and dagger that's going on, let me expand upon my Boxing In Bitcoin theory. As you'll recall from chapter 1, it posits that sometime in early 2021, the Fed began an operation to control the Bitcoin market for an indefinite length of time. They established a clandestine constellation of operatives that could purchase and sell Bitcoin and Bitcoin derivatives. Mathematically, this makes perfect sense. Here are five data points that support a high probability of successfully boxing in Bitcoin:

1. Bitcoin has a fixed set of units (21 million).
2. Bitcoin is mostly traded by retail customers.
3. The Fed's supply of U.S. dollars is virtually limitless.
4. The Fed's partner, the SEC, will only allow a Bitcoin futures market and will probably not approve a spot ETF until they are confident the company running the ETF will cooperate with their market manipulation.
5. In 2020, the SEC filed a lawsuit against the cryptocurrency company Ripple, alleging the firm sold XRP as an unregistered security. The XRP coin's sole purpose is to compete against the U.S. SWIFT international bank wire transfer system. The SEC has since appealed the case to higher courts.

Considering these five factors, the control of Bitcoin is academic. What is the outcome?

Suppress the price of Bitcoin but keep it alive—in a never-ending price range for decades. They don't care where the range or price is, just so they know how to keep it boxed and caged, but they can never kill it.

By early 2021, the Fed had lined up all five of these factors. The next necessary step was acquiring at least forty-five days of trading volume. That means, if on average 1,000 Bitcoins exchange hands per day, then the Fed would need to acquire 45,000 Bitcoins. If the average daily volume was 10,000 Bitcoins, then the Fed would need to acquire 450,000 Bitcoins. Either way, such massive spending was designed as a form of control.

Scan the QR code to watch the author explain how to control the Bitcoin market once the Fed owns forty-five days of trading volume.

The Boxing In Bitcoin theory posits that during June 2021, the Fed started purchasing Bitcoin at roughly a $30,000 level, causing prices to rise as they were acquiring their goal of forty-five days of trading volume. My best guess is that the quota was reached in November 2021 when Bitcoin reached its all-time high of approximately $69,000. The Fed's accumulation of Bitcoin was sending its price through the roof. As it happened, the conclusion of the Fed's activity came within weeks of both Bitcoin hitting an all-time high and the Bitcoin futures market opening for trading. The following six things all lined up in November 2021.

1. Speaking at an economic forum, former presidential candidate Hillary Clinton says Bitcoin "has the potential for undermining currencies, for undermining the role of the dollar as the reserve currency, [and] for destabilizing nations."[*]
2. Bitcoin prices hit an all-time high.
3. The SEC allows ETF Bitcoin futures (options) to start trading.
4. The SEC rejects a request to allow an ETF to actually trade Bitcoin.
5. Bitcoin starts an uncharacteristic trading pattern range.
6. The SEC's lawsuit against Ripple (XRP) is extended for no apparent reason. (Note, this lawsuit was partially lost in the summer of 2023 and then the SEC appealed to a higher court.)

FED LOADS UP ON BITCOIN IN 2021

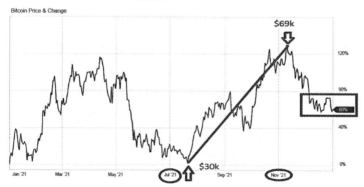

Bitcoin Price & Change

---

[*] Macauley Peterson, "Hillary Clinton: Crypto Has Potential for 'Undermining the Role of the Dollar as the Reserve Currency'," Blockworks, November 19, 2021, https://blockworks.co/news/hillary-clinton-crypto-has-potential-for-undermining-the-role-of-the-dollar-as-the-reserve-currency.

These facts lead to several conclusions, some less speculative than others:

- This operation was a team effort of the U.S. government, the U.S. Securities & Exchange Commission (SEC), and the Fed. The operation was similar to when President Roosevelt, the SEC, and the Fed outlawed gold ownership in May 1933.
- By November 2021, the Fed, and their covert operatives, had accumulated forty-five days of trading volume in Bitcoin—all happening within weeks of each other.
- The Fed's diabolical operations (administered by an unknown third-party organization) began manipulating the futures prices while also selling Bitcoin on the open market in a non-aggressive posture.
- Bitcoin, strangely, (and I am rounding percentages here) traded in an uncharacteristic range. Up 1 percent, down 2 percent, then up 1 percent back to its starting place. Then it happened again, up 1 percent, down 2 percent, then up 1 percent back to its original price. This identical up-and-down happened over and over. Money that was supposed to be outside of "the system." A store of wealth that cannot be controlled by anyone or any government, except . . . a government that has an unlimited supply of the world's reserve currency.

These and other factors open up a staggering array of possibilities. The following is one such hypothetical.[*]

---

[*] I am rounding out numbers here for illustrative purposes.

Starting in November 2021 and using the supply of forty-five days of trading volume previously acquired, our merry band of conspirators sells aggressively at $69,000, hawking their forty-five-day supply until they exhaust potential purchasers. With an operation like this, the chances of prices going higher are paper thin. When true-blue Bitcoin traders lose hope or doubt their own trading charts, they then begin to sell. The price drops to $66,000, and the Fed starts purchasing Bitcoin again, replenishing its forty-five days of trading volume supply.

But they're not done yet. Not by a long shot.

When buyers are convinced Bitcoin is not going lower—since there is a big buyer at $66,000—retail traders start purchasing and the demand for Bitcoin increases. Prices rise and the Fed uses its forty-five days of volume to sell non-aggressively at $68,000. But they don't allow Bitcoin to jump back to $69,000. That would be a bullish buy prompt for retail purchasers. Instead, they're hesitant, suspecting that Bitcoin has gone as high as it can. Accordingly, retail traders start selling to cover their position.

You can guess what happens next. As the selling begins again, the Fed steps in and starts purchasing Bitcoin at $65,000, replenishing its forty-five days of volume. Retailers' charts show that someone is buying Bitcoin, retail customers start buying once more, and prices increase again. Here, the Fed stakes a price ceiling of $67,000, producing yet another chart suggesting a Bitcoin high lower than the previous one—another bearish indicator. Selling ensues.

All this amounts to a slow, methodical, academic tug of war, leveraging unlimited U.S. dollars to eat away at the resolve of retail customers, over and over again. With this, Bitcoin is slowly being boxed in, caged, and the Fed's campaign eventually reduces Bitcoin's market cap from $1 trillion down to $400 billion. Broken down further, from $69,000 per coin, down to $36,000 per coin, and then down to $20,000 per coin. What is different from October 2021? Bitcoin's enemy has unlimited funds and is not the least interested in making a profit. It's nasty going up against that kind of adversary! *Fun Fact #1:* One billion seconds is 31.7 years. People underestimate how large the number "one billion" really is. I tell you this to preload my next fun fact.

Fun Fact #2: To push interest rates to almost 0 and compete against the negative interest rate bonds in Europe, the Fed purchased $120 billion of U.S. bonds **each month for thirty months.** Bitcoin's total market cap is only around $500 billion. Boxing In Bitcoin is not so difficult for an entity that has virtually unlimited financial resources.

What All This Can Teach Us

By now, I trust you agree with me that this entire situation of the U.S. government and Bitcoin manipulation certainly has its share of surreptitious, diabolical elements. To a degree, it's one of those story lines that, if you watched it in a movie, you'd be tempted to dismiss it as implausible, as way too farfetched.

But whether you fully buy into the Boxing In Bitcoin scenario or not, there's no disputing that it's a story loaded with valuable ideas and insights—there is knowledge illustrated here that we can all put to good use in our professional and financial lives. These institutions wield their power to manipulate markets and circumstances we're living in, so why can't we use some of what we're observing for our own benefit?

First off, a quick reminder: The purpose of this chapter is not to make any specific predictions regarding Bitcoin. It isn't meant to provide immediate direction or suggestions to influence your own portfolio decisions. Rather, I just want to provide the other side of the story—an alternative perspective of Bitcoin and an assessment of the strength of its enemies. I want to discuss what I see as the Fed's hidden agenda, which we can learn something from. No one can predict the future. All we can do is run probability tables and make decisions based upon those assumptions and information. Armed with this information, you can draw your own conclusions as to Bitcoin's future.

What's the probability that the Bitcoin market has, in fact, been placed in a cage? Eighty-five percent? Fifty percent? On the other hand, do you still feel reasonably confident that Bitcoin's value will skyrocket in the future? This is similar to what silver and gold buyers believed during a decade of JPMorgan's manipulation. Is this confidence in Bitcoin something you want to incorporate into your business, organization, or personal life? Again, run the probabilities and make your choices based on those probabilities. That being said, no matter your conclusion about Bitcoin, consider a number of valuable and insightful lessons provided by the Bitcoin story.

One such lesson harkens back to a phrase I used at the outset of this chapter—*price is a language*. It always has a story to tell, one that is as useful to a Nobel Prize–winning economist as it is to someone who's never cracked an economics book in their life. In the case of Bitcoin, price movement—virtually an orchestrated dance—tells a compelling tale of systematic control, of employing powerful forces at your disposal to dictate a currency's future and every movement.

The core message: Pay attention to price, no matter the setting or the circumstances. Price can reveal central objectives, motivation, and methodology, and in turn it can help you make decisions that best position you for financial success.

Back in chapter 1, I offered four statements, only one of which was true:

1. The Fed does not even care about Bitcoin.
2. The Fed would never try or even want to control Bitcoin.
3. The Fed does not view Bitcoin as a threat to the U.S. dollar.
4. The number one job of the Fed is to protect and promote the U.S. dollar.

Unto itself, price alone reveals which one of the four is an absolute fact.

The next lesson nicely transitions from the issue of price. Just as the Fed did, it's not necessary, or frankly even viable, to kill any competitor—real or imagined. With regard to the negative interest rate bonds discussed earlier, could the U.S. government simply "kill" them? Of course not. But what it could do is control them by lowering interest rates to a level so cheap that the dollar remained the go-to currency throughout the world.

Can the government kill the Bitcoin market? Maybe, but that's not really the point. Rather, as we've examined, it prefers to control it, dictate its price movement—there's price again!—and establish strict operating parameters. If nothing else, killing off Bitcoin would only likely prompt the creation of another competitor. Far better to control the one that's already there—an adversary it knows inside and out.

Watch for precursors. By that I mean something that has occurred in the past that bears a striking resemblance to something taking place in the present day. To illustrate—how did I identify one possible strategy with which the federal government can box in Bitcoin and keep it there for years to come? Easy—as discussed in chapter 1, I remembered JPMorgan did the very same thing only a few years before with the precious metals market. I looked for the precursor. I looked for the event that resembled what I was observing in the now.

The next lesson may seem to contradict a rule of thumb I suggested earlier—pay attention to what people do, not just what they say. That's certainly true. Keep your antennae up, acquiring clues, a sentence, or a remark for further insight.

Cue Hillary Clinton, November 2021, warning that the rise of Bitcoin and cryptocurrencies could undermine the U.S. dollar's reserve currency status. Unto itself, that would be a thought-provoking remark. But take it in the context of what happened just a mere several weeks later:

- Bitcoin hits an all-time high and then declines.
- Bitcoin begins to trade in an uncharacteristic range.
- A Bitcoin futures market opens up (once again, trading just in futures, not the coins themselves).
- The SEC's lawsuit against Ripple (XRP) is extended.

Add to those significant precursors the additional evidence discussed earlier:

- Tax U.S. citizens and require all taxes to be paid in U.S. dollars.
- Require crude oil transactions worldwide to be conducted exclusively with U.S. dollars.
- Require the SWIFT system (bank-to-bank transfers) to transact in only U.S. dollars.
- Offer irresistible low-interest loans available worldwide that must be repaid in U.S. dollars.

Taking all this into account, be certain to pay heed to what people and organizations do rather than what someone says when they open their mouths. But should they happen to say something that connects to and correlates with significant actions and events, that's talk worth bending an ear toward. Sometimes, the most powerful forms of confession are inadvertent.

No predictions, just probabilities. And it's highly probable that the U.S. government's actions regarding Bitcoin have a lot to teach us—whether you're interested in Bitcoin itself or not.

BOXING IN BASICS

3A. Never try to predict the future. Instead, calculate probabilities and possibilities.

3B. In business and in your life, take the time to know your opponent as thoroughly as possible.

3C. As the Bitcoin story shows, there's no need to destroy an opponent to win. Eliminating an opponent may only create a brand-new one. Often, merely controlling an adversary is just as effective.

3D. Price is a language. Follow it, study it, and it will always have a story to tell.

3E. Try not to judge too much when looking for role models. Did the U.S. government like what JPMorgan did? Probably not, but they went to school on it. Rather than standing knee-deep in the ocean with their hands extended trying to stop a wave from hitting the beach, they got a surfboard and rode it.

3F. Watch for precursors. The past, like price, often has a great deal to teach us.

3G. Watch the action of others instead of relying 100 percent on what they say.

CHAPTER 4
Reinventing the U.S. Dollar

If you don't reinvent, prepare to be marginalized. Success requires reinventing yourself. To stay relevant, Arnold Schwarzenegger had to reinvent himself three times. First as the most successful body-builder of his time, second as a Hollywood movie star, and third by becoming governor of California. Successful spouses reinvent themselves to build successful marriages. Successful businesses reinvent themselves to stay on top.

Scan the QR code to watch the author discuss
the reinvention of the U.S. dollar.

Perhaps most pertinent to our topic, the greatest product of all time also reinvented itself—in 1933, 1944, and 1971—and it will soon execute a reboot, transforming into the U.S. digital dollar.

Take a leap with me into the not-too-distant future:

The year is 2033. The U.S. government just outlawed all transfer of wealth unless it is transferred using the U.S. digital dollar. Cash is a thing of the past; possession of gold and silver is illegal. Purchasing products using Bitcoin or any other cryptocurrency is also illegal.

Sounds outrageous? To refresh your memory, a similar event happened in May 1933 when President Franklin D. Roosevelt and the U.S. government made it illegal for any U.S. citizen to own gold coins or gold bars. See the notice below, published in 1933.

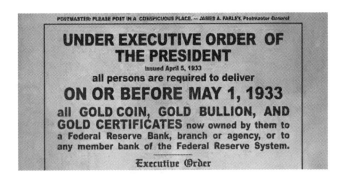

Scan the QR code to watch the author discuss the gold confiscation of 1933.

Regarding the digital dollar of tomorrow, understand that the public will probably vote with their social media platforms to have these types of laws and restrictions implemented for the good of the country—popular demand, 100 percent patriotic. In the eyes of the voter, this will be seen as absolutely the right thing to do. As in 1933, the U.S. public was probably convinced that turning in your gold was patriotic, and anyone who didn't comply was hurting the country. Therefore, the future American mindset may decide that this government-sanctioned monopoly is critical to the nation's safety and security. To understand how, let's return to the present day with an eye to the future.

From my perspective, this is how the digital dollar adoption will go. The government will use a four-phase campaign. The average American citizen will be persuaded that implementing a U.S. digital dollar is the only way to save the country's dominance on the world stage. Patriots will eventually be convinced that this "reset" is a sound and stable plan. They will even be impatient for it all to take place.

"Is it just me or does it bother anyone else that the board game Monopoly is manufactured by one single company? That just does not seem right, does it?" —Steven Wright, comedian

The manipulation will be carried out using the following four phases:

Phase 1: U.S. Digital Dollar Conversion Campaign— Resistance Is Futile

"All Americans, listen up! We are introducing a new way to pay for goods and services. It is called the U.S. digital dollar. It's similar to using cash. From this day forward all currency transactions can be accomplished by using cash and/or the new U.S. digital dollar. In the coming months, most Americans will discover that using the new digital dollar has many advantages over cash, but it is not the government's job to tell you which one to use. As Americans, you are free to choose. Use cash or the new U.S. digital dollar—either one is fine with us. No worries!"

The trap is now set.

There will be a strong marketing effort to prove the advantages of this "improved" form of currency. The government may offer incentives to switch. Although it will require a few years to build momentum and gain acceptance, citizens will come around to the advantage of U.S digital dollars over U.S. cash. After all, it's easy to use, efficient, and it mitigates theft. Just hold up your smartphone to a business's scanner, and—*ding*—the payment is complete. Two clicks on the phone and—*ding*—you transfer money to your kids in their U.S. digital dollar account. It is so easy, so simple, and so efficient that everyone will naturally just flow with it. Once adoption is reasonably mainstream, the government will launch phase two of the conversion campaign.

Phase 2: Manufacture a Crisis

A serious crisis will emerge. The U.S. government is going broke, primarily because many Americans do not pay their taxes in full. If all Americans did, the country would have no financial problems. In particular, one culprit is cash. Using cash for goods and services under the table allows citizens to dodge taxes. (This obviously is not the only reason—America is going broke because Congress spends too much money.) The manufactured crisis intensifies, and a blockchain-based currency (the USDD) can fix all of that.

The campaign will grow, spreading the word through various media about how the use of cash is crippling the American way. The loss of tax dollars from tax cheaters will become an accompanying national crisis. Popular news shows such as *60 Minutes* will flood us with images of damaged and outdated bridges and roads—dangers caused by tax dodgers dealing in cash. Homeless people and starving children will be shown repeatedly—hopeless victims of unpatriotic Americans wriggling out of their obligation to pay their fair share. If they did "The Right Thing," there would be no hungry children and not a single fellow citizen sleeping on a bench with a pile of newspapers for blankets.

Phase 2 will require several years of continuous fermentation. Congress will consider a parade of legislation aimed at addressing the situation, hoping to solve the repeated financial shortfalls of a government that spends more than it receives each year.

If only there was a solution to just collect the taxes that are owed! A method that ensures everyone pays their fair share. If we could solve this, we wouldn't have *any* financial problems and would remain the strongest country in the world.

Eureka! A new idea appears to fix everything, one that leverages an already burgeoning currency system. The USDD blockchain. A solution that guarantees all owed taxes will be paid, brimming with patriotism and a sense of fairness. All we have to do is implement this idea.

Phase 3: Vilify the Use of Cash

Now it's time for an even bolder campaign. Since the assumption is that people who use cash must also be tax dodgers who weaken America, a social media blitz of humiliation will take aim at any individuals providing services who often accept cash as payment. The argument will also be made that illegal activities like drug sales will be suppressed if we have a fully adopted USDD. Further, businesses that accept cash are allowing tax dodgers to continue the scam, weakening America further. Boycotting businesses that accept cash will become a popular protest for all patriotic citizens—that is, until a business capitulates and converts to 100 percent U.S. digital dollar transactions. "Patriotic" businesses will not accept cash, enabling their social media approval to climb.

This phase will snowball very fast. Levels of shame will reach fanatical levels as everyday people line up at their banks to convert their cash into the digital dollar. Others will withdraw their cash in physical form and hide it under their beds, but the question is, Where can they spend it without being shamed? But for the citizen whose conversion is completed, the individual will post on social media that they are now fully converted to USDD, and their friends will give them hundreds of "likes." Their social score will rise as they boast about having an account directly with the Fed.

Cash will still be legal tender, but it will be greatly discouraged—a financial scarlet letter. To discourage the use of cash, the government may stop issuing $100, $50 and $20 bills. Go to your bank for a withdrawal—they only have $1, $5, and $10 bills. Because using cash implies that you are an enemy of the United States of America.

Still think the government would never be able convince the public of this? Shake hands with the New York Gas Tax Scam of 1976.

Taxes? Oh, They're in the Mail . . .

The year was 1976. Michael Franzese had dropped out of college a few years earlier to join the family business—organized crime.*

Michael's father had been in this business for decades in New York City, and making a name for himself with notorious mob bosses and syndicated crime families was the goal.

But back in 1976, young Michael developed a brilliant plan that became one of the most successful financial scams that organized crime in the United States has ever concocted. This scam involved no illegal drugs, no prostitution, no murders, and no illegal gambling. As Michael put it: "We were just stealing from the government that stole from us."

It's now referred to as the New York Gas Tax Scam of 1976. Here's how it worked:

Michael and some friends would purchase a local gas station. At this time, local gas stations were responsible for collecting taxes and sending them to the state at the end of each month. Here's an example: Each month a local station would purchase gas from a gasoline wholesaler at $0.50 per gallon. The station would then sell gasoline for $1.05 a gallon. The profit cut was $0.50 to pay applicable taxes, $0.50 to pay for the actual gas, and $0.05 for the profit going to the local gas station owner. Out of $1.05 purchase, $0.50 went to taxes.

Each gas station owner had a bank account set up to collect and hold these tax premiums. The owners would remit tax payments monthly to the appropriate government agencies and duly report

---

* It should be noted that Michael Franzese has long since left a life of crime. He's the author of several books and made-for-TV shows discussing his life as a member of the mob.

their taxes. Michael and his buddies did things differently. Rather than paying tax money owed at the end of each month, they would just pocket the tax revenue and go on selling gasoline. This would continue for three months, at which point government agencies would mail them a very nice letter asking where the tax revenue was. Michael and crew would draft an equally nice letter back— always typed on very fancy company letterhead—saying that their accountant had been deathly ill and had been out of the office for several months. "Please forgive our tardiness. We'll get those funds to you immediately."

This exchange escalated for about nine months into a genuine cat-and-mouse game. Eventually, state officials would decide to make a personal visit to the gas station. Fortunately for Michael, he and his crew had a guy on the inside who would tip them off that government officials were on their way.

The night before their arrival, Michael's operatives would board up the gas station, close the doors, and paint "Out of Business" signs on the outside. When the state officials raided the empty gas station the next morning, Michael's attorney would simultaneously be at the courthouse filing bankruptcy papers for that financially struggling little gas station. Months later, when the gas station was sold at a bankruptcy auction, Michael's "Cousin Anthony" would somehow be the highest bidder. A few weeks later, it was open for business under different ownership, selling gasoline again, not paying taxes, and waiting for a letter from the state officials that should arrive in about ninety days. Nine months later, they would file bankruptcy with another cousin waiting in the wings to buy it back at bankruptcy auction.

Michael's enterprise eventually had hundreds of gas stations across New York. The scam was so good, New York state regulators simply could not catch them. Finally, they had to petition state legislators to change the laws, requiring gasoline wholesalers to collect the tax. Leaving it up to individual station owners was costing the state millions.

Did the new law end the scam? Anything but. As Michael says, "We couldn't believe our luck. We were so tired of running hundreds of gas stations. It was too much work." Instead, they went out and purchased a gas wholesaler. The new law allowed them to scale up their business. They made way more money and expanded quickly. Why? They continued to pocket gas tax money and, as a result, could sell gasoline cheaper than all the other wholesalers. Why? Because they did not pay taxes!

They even went international. Michael set up a bunch of different gas wholesale companies in Panama. When regulators caught on to the scam, Franzese's operatives would close one Panama corporation and move it to another Panama corporation, all set up and ready to go. It was a perfect "daisy chain."

After paying the lion's share of the scam to all the crew chiefs and mob bosses, Michael Franzese was still personally raking in approximately $30 million per month, tax free. This scam ran for years—it was the most profitable scam any organized crime family has ever perpetrated in the United States.

By the year 2033, stories like the Gas Tax Scam of 1976 will easily convince the everyday U.S. citizen to wholeheartedly convert 100 percent to the USDD. After all, the country will be on the brink of financial disaster, thanks to a dependence on and loopholes of a cash-based system.

Phase 4: Crush All Competitors of the U.S. Digital Dollar

Here's the endgame. In May 2033 (the one-hundred-year anniversary of gold confiscation), the only transfer of wealth or currency allowed in the U.S.A. must be the U.S. digital dollar. All other forms of payment—Bitcoin, cash, gold, and silver—will be illegal. Why? Because all other methods allow for un-American tax dodgers to weaken the country.

Tax returns will be a thing of the past, as will banks as most of us know them. With a 100 percent digital and mandatory blockchain currency, there will be no need to file a tax return on April 15 each year. Instead, a few nickels will immediately be transferred to the Fed or the U.S. Treasury each time you purchase an item. Taxes will be collected electronically every time a financial transaction takes place. Will it be up-to-the-minute tax collection? Hardly. It will be up-to-the-nanosecond tax collection. A perfect world!

There will be other advantages. The system will allow the government to change tax rates throughout the country. Moreover, there will be endless opportunities for social tinkering. Need to mitigate the proliferation of sugar-caused diabetes? Instantly raise the taxes on all sugary drinks in America by 25 percent. Need to raise taxes on all goods made in China? Just change the tax codes for those items. Made-in-America products may be taxed at 17 percent and made-in-China products at 37 percent. All controlled by Washington, D.C. Need to boost American milk farmers? Lower the tax on 2 percent whole milk to a mere 2 percent sales tax.

This will amount to an ultimate power grab, allowing unprecedented control by the government. And most Americans will be willing to accede to this new authority, all in the name of "patriotism" and seeming fair play. Not surprisingly, problems will crop up.

Once implemented, citizens will slowly realize that they have given up most of the freedom they grew up with. The freedom they love. The freedom they believe is their inalienable birthright. The freedom they thought they were protecting by buying into the U.S. digital dollar.

Then again . . .

You want a heart transplant? We couldn't help but notice that you've bought pancakes dripping with butter and syrup and two extra-large sodas every day for the past five years. Why would we grant your surgery request when you've done this to yourself? Your sense of personal responsibility—as reflected in your social media score—is simply not high enough to warrant a heart transplant.

Still, the government will continually seek to create insatiable demand and mess with your mind. To make digital dollars even more enticing, the government may introduce universal income for the average U.S. citizen. A thousand dollars is deposited into every citizen's account, each and every month! How sweet is that!? This would only be available to the majority of middle-class and poor citizens.

But the money has a time-bomb attached. The recipient must spend it in the next thirty days, or it will be automatically withdrawn from their account electronically. Additionally, it can only be used to purchase made-in-America products to serve as a short-term stimulus to the economy.

If your apartment rent each month is less than $500, the rent payment to your landlord will include a 3 percent transfer to the Fed for taxes. But if rent is $2,500, that means *luxury*—and luxury costs. You may pay upwards of 30 percent in sales taxes. Luxury boats—tack on a 50 percent sales tax.

Every single transfer of currency will be taxed. Move cash to your children's account so they can pay for a hamburger at a high school football game—taxes withdrawn. If currency moves anywhere, anytime, taxes or fees must be paid. All other forms of financial transactions will be illegal.

As if that weren't enough, this system will give the government real-time access to all your bank accounts. No more offshore or hidden Swiss stashes. Everyone will have a U.S. Federal Reserve Bank account, or at least a bank account with one of the twelve Federal Reserve banks across the country.

In fact, the adoption of Phase 4 may even resemble an old biblical prophecy:

> *And he causeth all, both small and great, rich and poor, free and bond, to receive a mark in their right **hand**, or in their foreheads: And that **no man might buy or sell**, save he that had the mark, or the name of the beast, or the **number** of his name.* —Revelation 13: 16-17 (KJV) [Emphasis added.]

All freedom will be gone. Your Federal Reserve bank account number will be all you need. Don't have one? Food, gas, and shelter will be unattainable. This number will need to be memorized in your forehead or written in your hand-held phone. Without it, you'll be neutralized in every manner—a subservient beast that can be controlled by the whims of a government.

Still think this can't happen, that it's too farfetched? It already has.

Computer Chip Implants under the Skin

Welcome to the future! As reported by CBS News in 2017, a Wisconsin technology company is offering its employees microchip implants that can be used to scan into the building and purchase food at work. The plan involves implanting employees with micro-chips the size of grains of rice that function as swipe cards—to open doors, operate printers, or buy smoothies at the company cafeteria with a wave of the hand.

"The biggest benefit, I think, is convenience," said the company's co-founder and chief executive, whose name was deleted for privacy. "It basically replaces a lot of communication devices—whether it be credit cards or keys." And, naturally enough, this is all up to the individual employee. Get one or not. It's all up to you. Sound familiar?

Still, there will likely be many citizens who don't think technolog-ical advancements like this are the greatest idea ever. They'll preserve their freedom by growing their own food, raising chickens and beef, milking cows, and manufacturing their own electricity from wind or solar power. All for personal use, with no need to transfer money to anyone else—hence, no need for a U.S. digital dollar account number.

Unfortunately, they may not be as safely independent as they believe they are. The fact is, in the past, the U.S. government has repeatedly used the U.S. Constitution's "Commerce Clause" (Article 1, Section 8, Clause 3) to thwart this type of self-reliance. Moreover, the courts have consistently supported the government in its enforcement of this clause. (The Commerce Clause paradox will be explained in Chapter 5.)

Even though this off-the-grid approach will be extremely difficult to execute, some stalwarts will try, nonetheless. And most will be, in the end, unsuccessful and succumb to the massive forces and real power of the U.S. government.

To reinforce: This discussion is purely hypothetical. It is a *theory*. That does not mean it eventually will be real. Predicting the future is a very difficult task—impossible, if you ask me. But providing probabilities of the future creates outcomes that may

NOTE TO SELF
Go with the Flow

Before my supersized business can become fully grown, it will need to reinvent itself several times. Therefore, don't fight the change, flow with it.

be relied on. It is not unlikely that portions of this hypothesized future reality could make their way into our true reality one day, and thinking in this way is what allows us to make our best guesses in predicting the best choices for ourselves today.

Still, the U.S. digital dollar is coming—when and how fast, we are not sure. In November 2022, the Fed announced it would partner with Wells Fargo Bank and Citibank to test a U.S. digital currency. It's very likely we will see this in our lifetime. That's because the U.S. government needs to execute a reset like it did in May 1933 by outlawing the ownership of gold. Or a reset similar to the 1944 Bretton Woods Agreement making the U.S. dollar a world-dominating currency. And the reset in 1971 to the petrodollar. A reset is coming—when is the only question.

Why? One hundred percent of all fiat currencies have eventually gone to 0. How likely is it the U.S. dollar proves the exception to the rule? Decide this on your own. Remember that predicting the future is almost impossible, but running probabilities to increase the chances of success is what astute humans seek to do.

To be the number one product of all time, reinvention is a necessity, not an anomaly or one of many options. This simple school lesson has been implemented by famous people, marriages, businesses, and entrepreneurs. It is part of the success formula. The rise and dominance of the U.S. dollar is a perfect case study, as it cannot be ignored when shooting for success. Reinvent or face destruction—make way for the USDD.

When I raised my children, my plan was to be three different types of parents. When my boys were younger than twelve years old, I was a 100 percent parent. Between twelve and twenty years old, I changed my persona to being a parent 70 percent of the time and their friend 30 percent of the time. After twenty years old, I was their friend 70 percent and their parent 30 percent of the time. Similar to Arnold Schwarzenegger's three careers, I had three stages of my parenting career. If you are an entrepreneur in the United States, the company under your control will probably need to reinvent itself several times for it to remain relevant and successful.

Seek to learn from successful people, successful products such as the U.S. dollar, and successful businesses. We can glean from their success. And reinvention may be one of the most important lessons that cannot be ignored.

BOXING IN BASICS

4A. Successful individuals and organizations repeatedly reinvent themselves to stay successful. Follow their lead. Otherwise, prepare to be marginalized.

4B. The U.S. dollar—the number one product on the planet—has undergone several reinventions.

4C. Probability suggests the United States will adopt a digital dollar system in the future. Can you fight it, or is it more prudent to leverage it to your advantage?

4D. If you agree that the country is destined to adopt a digital dollar, watch for signs that suggest steps toward that end. What do they involve, and can you use any of that information to your benefit?

CHAPTER 5
The Commerce Clause

If the U.S. government can make owning gold illegal, like they did in May 1933, then the obvious question becomes: What *can't* they do?

"Should do" or "should not do" versus "cannot do" are totally different concepts. If in 1932, you told me that next year the U.S. government would put me in jail if I did not cash in my gold, I would have said it was impossible. I would have been dead wrong, as it was possible—it just wasn't *probable*.

The year 1933 was evidence, and a lesson, of what the U.S. government can do. When owning gold bullion, coins, or bars becomes illegal, then the possibilities of government control explode exponentially. Being forced to trade something tangible of high perceived value—gold—for a piece of paper just doesn't seem like the American way. We believe we are free in this country. This is true . . . until the government wants or needs what you have. Then and only then what you deem "impossible" is redefined, and legal documents morph into perspectives that deny their very definition.

The Commerce Clause

Within the U.S. Constitution there is a clause—the Interstate Commerce Clause—written "to regulate commerce between the States, foreign Nations, and Indian Tribes." It is a federal law by design, intended to protect the interests of the American people—that is, until the government wants what you have. Then the interpretation of the law is stretched so far that it bends the mind and grinds on our sense of fairness.

In the 1942 case of *Wickard v. Filburn*, 317 U.S. 111, an Ohio farmer (Mr. Filburn) grew wheat to feed his farm animals. Previously, the U.S. government had established limits on wheat production based on the Commerce Clause. These caps were calculated according to the acreage owned by the farmer, enabling the stabilization of wheat prices and supplies across America.

Mr. Filburn farmed additional wheat—more than the amount that was permitted. When the government fined him, he argued that his wheat was not sold to anyone and was only used for his own animals' consumption. That, he said, by definition could not be regulated as commerce—let alone "interstate commerce."

"Growing wheat for my own animals on my own land simply is not commerce," Mr. Filburn contended.

That appears to be a strong argument. The words cited by Mr. Filburn seemed to have been very clearly defined historically. That is, until there was motivation to change definitions or meanings of the original intent of laws in favor of the U.S. government. Everything is copacetic until the U.S. government wants what you have.

The U.S. Supreme Court decided against Mr. Filburn. If you remember that this involves the Constitution's Commerce Clause, it seems all the more dramatically unsound when used against a single wheat farmer growing food with which to feed his own livestock. But, when it needs or wants to, the federal government holds all the cards to increasing its power.

When I think of this particular case, I remember the joke that the late comedian George Carlin told, comparing different words in football and baseball:

- Football is played on a "gridiron." Baseball is played on a "diamond" in a park.
- Football has a "two-minute warning." Baseball has a "seventh-inning stretch."
- Footballs can go "out of bounds." Some baseballs are not bad balls, they're just a little bit "foul."

The U.S. government does not "break" laws. It just "bends" them by changing definitions of words when it best suits its needs. Moreover, the highest court in the country readily validated its actions.

In the case of Mr. Filburn, the Supreme Court stated that "whether the subject of the regulation in question was 'production,' 'consumption,' or 'marketing' is, therefore, not material for purposes of deciding the question of federal power before us . . . But even if appellee's activity be local and though it may not be regarded as commerce, it may still, whatever its nature, be reached by Congress if it exerts a **substantial economic effect on interstate commerce** and this irrespective of whether such effect is what might at some earlier times have been defined as 'direct' or 'indirect.'" [Emphasis added.]

Essentially, from the government's perspective, Mr. Filburn's wheat-growing activities reduced the total quantity of wheat he would buy for his animal feed on the market. That, in turn, affected interstate commerce.

Effectively, Mr. Filburn had to pay a fine for *not* purchasing wheat. Wow!

This decision is possibly the most far-reaching example of the Commerce Clause's specific authority over intrastate business and trade. Perhaps more important, it greatly expanded the authority of Congress well beyond the original definition in the Constitution.

The ripple effect of this decision has impacted other cases over the years. One example is medical marijuana. Consider this scenario: Someone is extremely sick, and medical marijuana can help them get through the day with more comfort and peace. Under the ruling of the Filburn case, if that person grows their own medical marijuana, they are not purchasing marijuana on the open market. Therefore, that affects price discovery, impacting the free market. The Supreme Court has relied heavily on the *Wickard v. Filburn* case to prosecute individuals who grow their own medicinal marijuana. They want these people to be purchasing their marijuana on the open market so the marijuana industry (and the government) gets their share.

Like Mr. Filburn, growing your own medical marijuana on your own property exclusively for personal consumption is somehow interpreted as "affecting interstate commerce." That makes no sense on many levels. For one thing, since it's not being transported anywhere, it should first be viewed as *intrastate* commerce. But, moreover, it should not be defined as "commerce" in the first place. There is no commerce occurring when you're cultivating your own materials.

Still, they've used that argument again and again. In 2005, the Supreme Court stated in *Gonzalez v. Raich* that, like homegrown wheat, homegrown medical marijuana is subject to federal regulation because it competes with medical marijuana that is bought and sold in interstate commerce. In effect, the court rulings established that Congress *can* regulate purely intrastate activity that is not itself "commercial"—in that it is not produced for sale—if it concludes that failure to regulate would undercut the regulation of the interstate market in that commodity.

Wow. Activities that are not commerce but which could affect intrastate commerce? That is what the Commerce Clause in the U.S. Constitution was meant to protect against when it was written into law!? *Bending a rule without breaking the law.* All that's needed is changing the definitions of written words.

In another case, the Commerce Clause was used to require a small barbeque restaurant in Alabama to end segregation in 1964. Ollie's Barbecue, owned by Ollie McClung in Birmingham, had more than two hundred seats in its restaurant—but they were for Caucasian customers only. African American customers could buy takeout orders, but they could not sit at the tables.

Katzenbach v. McClung, 379 U.S. 294 (1964) proved to be a landmark decision of the U.S. Supreme Court. In filing the suit, the family-owned restaurant argued it had a right to refuse service to anyone. Further, it contended that the restaurant could not be prohibited from discriminating against African Americans, because Congress did not have power under the Commerce Clause to enact the Civil Rights Act of 1964. (The act outlawed segregation based on race, color, religion, or national origin in all public accommodations engaged in interstate commerce, including restaurants.)

Therein lies the rub. As it happened, Ollie's Barbecue was located on a state highway close to an interstate highway. On average, half of the food it purchased was from local suppliers and half originated out of state. Ultimately, the Supreme Court used the Commerce Clause to rule against Ollie's Barbecue, forbidding racial discrimination by citing a burden to "interstate commerce." Their reasoning:

1. Half of the ingredients on the menu crossed state lines to get to Ollie's restaurant.
2. If people of African heritage were restricted to takeout as opposed to sitting in a restaurant, then they couldn't travel as freely and as easily from state to state to conduct interstate commerce.

Accordingly, the Court ruled unanimously that the Commerce Clause was properly applied with regard to Ollie's Barbecue.

In section 4 of the opinion, the Court held that racial discrimination in restaurants had a significant impact on interstate commerce. As such, Congress had the power to regulate this conduct under the Commerce Clause. The Court cited testimony that African Americans spent significantly less time in areas with racially segregated restaurants. Additionally, the Court noted that segregation imposed an artificial restriction on the flow of merchandise by discouraging African Americans from making purchases in segregated establishments. The Court gave the greatest weight to evidence that segregation in restaurants had a direct and highly restrictive effect upon interstate travel by African Americans, which was not supportive of a healthy and free-flowing economy. Additionally, the Court affirmed previous decisions that Congress has the authority to regulate local intrastate activities if the activities significantly affect overall interstate commerce.

The bottom line here was if legislators have a rational basis for finding a chosen regulatory scheme necessary to protect commerce, the Court will support them. I, for one, am glad the Court ruled against Ollie's for discrimination. Ollie's employed a morally wrong and grotesque policy of segregation in a country that sacrificed more than half a million people to abolish slavery. But what perplexes me is, why did the litigation use the Commerce Clause to stop Ollie's discrimination? In a country that has many laws addressing discrimination, why did they need to use a law that covers interstate commerce to achieve this result?

In using the three prior examples—the wheat farmer, homegrown marijuana, and a local barbecue restaurant—it's obvious the Commerce Clause has far-reaching applications when employed by the U.S. Supreme Court. Using the Commerce Clause to accomplish a moral, virtuous, and appropriate outcome against Ollie's is fantastic from my point of view. But this doesn't mean it isn't being used outside of its original written intent. Further, these cases illustrate how the United States could one day outlaw gold, Bitcoin, or silver.

Some argue that the U.S. government cannot control or make Bitcoin illegal—that there is no legal precedent to do so. But I am not sure that "cannot" applies here. When something threatens the number one product in the world, the U.S. government will find a chosen regulatory scheme necessary to protect commerce. End of argument!

This interpretation and implementation of the Commerce Clause is kind of like saying, "If a group of butterflies starts flapping their wings in Tennessee, then under the Commerce Clause, that could create windstorms in Arkansas that damage crops." It appears that the Commerce Clause is all-seeing, all-knowing, and transcends all commonly accepted definitions.

> NOTE TO SELF
> ## Know the Law
> Your supersized business idea is doomed if it does not have a good grasp of the U.S. legal system. Remember, it is a game with real financial rewards and also pitfalls.

Superman is nothing compared to the power of the Commerce Clause. Darth Vader may even agree that the Commerce Clause might even be more powerful than "The Force." But it also shows how boxing in your business in a similar fashion—meaning increasing the odds of its success—can prove just as powerful.

Let's Talk Chances

Does understanding the ramifications of the court cases we just discussed give you any insight into what the U.S. government will do to protect its number one product? Will Bitcoin replace the U.S. dollar in the near future? What are the chances? And if you say the chances are good, then do you really know how to assess and run probabilities, thereby giving yourself the best chances of success?

That's an important skill to have when driving a business toward the outcome you desire.

To help you out, let's play a game of chance. There is a single Bitcoin behind one of three doors. If you choose the correct door, you will be awarded one whole Bitcoin. Therefore, you have a 33.33 percent chance of the Bitcoin being behind door number one, a 33.33 percent chance of the Bitcoin behind door number two, and the same odds for door number three.

You choose door number two. Then our game show host announces we are going to increase your odds of winning by letting you choose again. We will eliminate door number one because the Bitcoin was not behind that door. Now there is door number two, which you selected. Door number three remains as a possible choice. Do you want to keep door number two as your choice or would you like to switch to door number three?

Here's the significant detail: Even though there are only two doors left, your chances are NOT 50/50. It may seem like a 50/50 chance, but it's not. If you stay with door number two, your chances of winning remain at 33.33 percent. But if you switch to door number three, your chances of winning rise to 66.66 percent. Okay, I am assuming you probably do not agree with my math. Let's do it one more time.

Same scenario, but now there are one hundred doors, and there is one Bitcoin behind one single door. You choose door number two, and therefore you have a 1 percent chance of being correct. Then the game show host says we are going to eliminate all the other ninety-nine doors except for one. Now the only two choices left are door number two and door number twenty-seven. It appears now to be a 50/50 chance of winning. But, once again, it is not.

You can stay with your choice of door number two, or you can switch to door number twenty-seven. What should you do? If you stay with door number two, your chances of winning are still only 1 percent. But if you switch to door number twenty-seven you have a 99 percent chance of winning. That's because it is NOT **just** two doors you are choosing from. You are choosing from two doors with a **history**—a perspective that goes further than just random chance. That is entirely different from choosing between just two doors that you know nothing about. In this scenario, you have a history. You have more information that can increase your chances of winning. It's not a guarantee, it just increases your probability to 99 percent if you now select door number twenty-seven.

This all assumes that the game is fair. But what if the game is rigged and by some stroke of luck the Bitcoin is actually behind door number two? Then the game show host knows this and is trying to trick you into switching your selection. If you change to door number twenty-seven and then lose, you would be understandably suspicious that the game was, in fact, rigged.

In a fair game, mathematics, charts, and other empirical facts make sense. They increase your probability of winning. But in a rigged game, the math would be misleading by design. From every chart and probability, Bitcoin should already be worth $100,000 or more, but that is not the case. Therefore, the price of Bitcoin is not being allowed to find "price discovery," which is a fundamental requirement of a free market. Why? Because the Fed is manipulating it.

If you are playing the real-life Bitcoin game, betting against the U.S. dollar, all I am asking is that you know how the game is played. What are the chances of success, who is the adversary, and what are their motives? Are they extremely powerful, and can they win by attrition? They may be able to win not because they are right or correct but because they may be able to be irrational longer than you can be solvent. Many battles in history are won simply by attrition: war, legal cases, divorces, and yes, finances.

Understanding the Commerce Clause may help your chances of winning the Bitcoin investing game. It's not a guarantee—it just improves the probabilities. I don't try to predict the future. I believe this is a fool's game. But I do like to run probabilities. *No predictions, just probabilities* becomes a formula for success and a path to creating luck. It is the formula I continually try to follow in life and business. Making conclusions based on evidence is what humans strive to do.

To my way of thinking, Bitcoin is the greatest idea in the world of money. But the very nanosecond that Bitcoin came into existence, it was destined to go up against the most powerful currency of all time. It was destined to battle with the Fed, in concert with the SEC, the

U.S. government, and the Navy—an extremely formidable opposition working as a united front to protect its number one product.

If you run the biblical story of David and Goliath over and over, Goliath wins 99 percent of the time. Bitcoin has a chance of winning, but is that chance in the short term or in the very distant future? A future so far away that it will be difficult for you or me to profit from it? A future that has to experience the emergence of the U.S. digital dollar, the elimination of cash, the worldwide market manipulations of Bitcoin and precious metals, and the replacement of the most prolific and powerful product ever created by human beings?

It is possible, but is it *probable*?

Once again: The epitome of ignorance is not believing in something based exclusively on the fact that you know nothing about that subject. Removing the word "cannot" from our vocabulary when speaking about the U.S. government will make any conversation more believable. "Cannot" is not the correct word. Conversations using possibilities versus probabilities are much more productive and effective. In fact, "cannot" and the U.S. government should probably never be used in the same sentence!

What can we learn from the Commerce Clause? The story of the Commerce Clause exhibits the possibilities of real-world history. And it shows just how far the government will go to protect its number one product of all time. There are only two positive things you can do with history—learn from it and forgive. All other things are negative. Because the Commerce Clause is such an unbelievably successful campaign, we must learn from it.

BOXING IN BASICS

5A. The U.S. government has repeatedly applied the Commerce Clause when it afforded necessary leverage. In the future, Bitcoin may have to battle with it.

5B. In protecting its number one product, the U.S. Supreme Court has applied interesting interpretations of the Commerce Clause to support the government.

5C. Whether accusing a wheat farmer of inhibiting commerce by growing food for his farm animals or ending segregation in an Alabama barbecue, the essential question has never come down to what the government *should* do. Rather, it's a matter of what it *can* do.

5D. What's your number one product? What will you do to protect it and nurture its growth?

PART TWO

Blue Jeans to Billions

CHAPTER 6

One Man's Trash Is Another Man's Startup

A sign that could only have come from heaven once told me in no uncertain terms to:

1. Plunge headfirst into a dumpster teeming with trash.
2. Quit my job and start a secondhand blue jeans business.

That sign was a stack of blue jeans. And, like the indicators derived from the campaign to box in Bitcoin, I only picked up on the message because my business antennae were fully extended, as always, searching for a signal.

By the mid-1980s, I knew in my heart that I needed to be my own boss—not just wanted but *needed*. The thought of sitting in front of my employer every year, allowing them to ponder if I deserved a 2 or 3 percent raise, suffocated my soul. I felt like a second grader in front of a stern teacher praying for a B instead of a B-minus. It was more than an issue of money—I needed to be in the driver's seat of my life. Subservient passenger status had no appeal.

Still, my attitude was optimistic. I never asked myself, *Why can't I start a business?* Rather, I asked a positive affirmation question of ***How can I*** *start a business?* was what I repeated in my mind continually.

Searching for a business to start is a lofty task. I faced problems—several of them. First and foremost was my lack of cash, which inhibited my ability to acquire or start a new enterprise. Moreover, I had a family—a wife, a one-year-old son, and another on the way. Supporting them with food, housing, and health insurance while taking on astronomical hours that went with going out on my own was all a huge risk. As Captain James T. Kirk of the starship *Enterprise* once said: "Risk . . . We are in the business of risk."

One evening at work in 1988, two colleagues and I grabbed a vacant conference room to review a business plan to acquire made-in-the-U.S.A. used Levi's 501 button-fly blue jeans and sell them in Eastern European countries. The agenda—deciding ownership structure, job responsibilities, how to finance the operation, and the time commitment—carried us late into the evening.

Despite our enthusiasm, we all faced the same challenges—full-time jobs and growing families to provide for. Any new enterprise would demand an enormous time commitment, draining moments we spend with our loved ones and straining our modest financial resources. We decided to sleep on it. The next day, we'd let each other know whether we were in or out.

I drove home to my small two-bedroom townhome about fifteen minutes away. Walking in the back door, I could hear my wife upstairs putting our son to bed. I saw an overflowing garbage can in the kitchen and commenced to carry the trash 50 yards through the parking lot toward a dumpster. Just as I was about to make the deposit, I spotted a stack of used denim blue jeans inside the large steel container.

Three seconds later I was waist-high in trash (my version of dumpster diving). With a quick calculation, I realized the stack of secondhand pants—soiled as they were—was worth two days' salary at my current job. I had no doubt that this was a genuine sign from heaven.

Come on, what are the odds? And from that very moment, I was in—and I was in *BIG*! No more dipping my toe in the water to check the temperature. No more enduring weekend seminars about a new franchise opportunity that I couldn't afford anyway. At that moment, I knew what I was supposed to do. I knew then that I had to focus entirely on the success of this used denim jeans venture.

There have been only a few moments in my lifetime when I was in the right place at the right time and—this is the important part—simultaneously knew exactly what to do. I realized in the moment the magnitude of the opportunity. This is truly an empowering feeling. It is also sobering. Because it meant that the only thing holding me back from success was my personal focus and effort. If I failed, it was all on me. I understood that anything less could leave me with years of regret, wondering if a lack of commitment and effort had doomed things from the start. As Saul Bellow famously wrote, it was time to "seize the day."

Call it destiny. Dismiss it as coincidence. I wasn't worried about what to label it. Let's light this firecracker and see where we land after it explodes. As we will see shortly, the blast from that firecracker carried me and my partners around the world, thanks in part to the largest, most well-constructed, and well-executed monopoly there has ever been—the U.S. dollar.

A Market Hungry for Jeans

Before 1989, there was very little commerce and trade between the Soviet Bloc and the western allies. However, new opportunities broke loose like a flood once the Soviets and the United States lowered their restrictive trade policies. Eastern European countries had been deprived of western goods for decades, and demand surged.

Here's a look at how that demand played out: If someone traveled to Moscow wearing denim jeans—especially a pair of American Levi's 501 button-fly jeans—teenagers in Moscow would casually approach and offer $100 for jeans that the Americans had bought at a fraction of the price. Tourists could literally pay for their trip if they brought a suitcase full of these denim Americana pants.

It's easy to see what fueled that. Although economic contact had been slight, Eastern European teenagers could still watch American TV and Hollywood movies. Whether on a talk show or a motion picture, the prevailing choice of cool was faded denim jeans made in the U.S.A. As these teenagers—like most teenagers throughout the world—drooled over the sight of these iconic clothes, their desire to look and dress like Hollywood stars only grew.

Additionally, the United States of America created a new economic wave in 1989 by being victors of the Cold War—and became beloved by the world community. Pretty much everybody on the globe wanted to wear original U.S.A. clothing. And there was nothing more original than the button-fly 501 denim pants made by Mr. Levi Strauss from San Francisco, California.

This was a wave I could ride. Growing up in Las Vegas in the 1980s, I and almost all my friends wore Levi's 501 button-fly denim jeans every day of the week. We wore them as work jeans or school pants. When they went on sale for $12.99, we would snatch up three or four pairs. These pants were a day-to-day necessity, like a loaf of bread.

In 1988, Levi Strauss & Co. started marketing the original 501 jean in New York, London, Munich, and Paris as a fashion item with a price of $80 up to $100. Since these jeans had been marketed in the western United States as work jeans for more than eighty years, they remained affordable in that particular market. This was a problem for Levi's, since it was effectively working against itself.

In the California Gold Rush in the mid-nineteenth century, men with shovels and dynamite mined for gold. But it was merchants who got rich as they shipped items from the eastern United States to California with an 800 percent markup. Recognizing that newly wealthy miners would gladly pay exorbitant prices, those merchants, using arbitrage and market timing, became wealthy.

In 1989, my partners and I decided to do the exact same thing— only going in the opposite direction. As there were hundreds of thousands of used Levi's 501s all over the western United States, all we had to do was mine them, clean them up, and ship them to Europe for a huge profit. Market timing and arbitrage, all over again.

Shortly after my epiphany in the dumpster, I quit my job and made used jeans my full-time endeavor. Six months later, my other partner quit his job and joined me full-time. The third partner received a really great job offer in another state and, somewhat regretfully, bowed out of the business. But a little over a year later, he rejoined the two of us as he moved his family to southern Germany and became the marketing and distribution arm of the company. And then it became not just fantastic but faaaaaantastic! Why? Because I had brilliant business partners. We worked as a team, and profits soared. It was a 100 percent American-greenback business, and it was selling like hotcakes.

Scan the QR code to watch a 1996 news interview with the author on the used Levi's denim jean business.

The Nuts and Bolts of the Business

Economics has a term called a "reverse demand curve." This phenomenon does not happen that often, as it's the direct opposite of a normal demand curve. As you probably know, a regular demand curve maps out supply versus demand. The greater the supply, the lower the price. A reverse demand curve means the greater the quantity, the greater the price. For instance, if you want to buy one Leonardo Da Vinci painting, the cost is $100,000. But if you want to purchase ten paintings at the same place and at the same time, the price jumps to $5 million. In effect, the greater the quantity, the greater the price.

Used Levi's 501 jeans had somewhat of a reverse demand curve. A person from Europe could come to America and purchase one pair of used Levi's 501 jeans at a thrift store for $6. But if that same person wanted to purchase 3,000 used Levi's 501 jeans at the same place at the same time, the price shot up to $21 each. Rather than a volume discount, a larger quantity only served to increase the cost.

Reverse demand curves require many events to converge at the same time to create such a strange economic phenomenon. In our case, one such factor was the inability of the Levi Strauss & Co. to raise their prices in the western United States to match other prices around the world. After all, the price had been established for eighty years. Additionally, U.S. President Ronald Reagan's call to Soviet Union President Mikhail Gorbachev to take down the wall in Germany was like pouring lighter fluid on our firecracker. For us, the demand and distribution opportunities skyrocketed.

We moved quickly and leveraged our spot in history to the max. With the one distribution hub established in southern Germany, I traveled to Barcelona, Spain, to organize a second. In particular, the Spanish teenage fashion magazines had taken hold of the overdye market. Here's how we handled it. When we had a used pair of stained pants that we couldn't clean, we removed the leather patch, dyed the jean jet black or dark navy blue, and sold it as an overdyed used Levi's 501 jean. As purchasing stained jeans from a thrift store cost us less than $1 per unit, the reclamation profit margins were enormous.

At the same time, we were also buying new jeans at department stores in the western United States. Levi's tried to stop this by limiting sales to two items per customer. Our solution—a vanload of kids who walked in and bought all the 501s the store had on the shelves, two at a time.

Levi Strauss wasn't done. To combat arbitrage and lost sales in Europe, the company raised their prices in the West so high that it squeezed our arbitrage margins. At first, I was furious. But this was a time in my life when I stopped to consider a wave of change larger than myself, and I grabbed a surfboard. After I reflected and paid attention, I could not believe our luck. Strauss's price increase caused the used market demand to soar even higher. By this time in the city of Berlin, a brand-new pair of Levi's 501 jeans was about $120, and a used pair was approximately $60 to $80.

Here's the math. Our company in the United States "sold" the pants to our company in southern Germany for anywhere from $21 to $23. The items were then sold to a European retail store for $31 to $35, which then marked the pants up to $60 to $80. Our company was surfing a wave that was only getting bigger.

It's All in How You Get Them

Business was booming—competitors began to emerge. Some of the largest were located in Los Angeles. Still, at the height of the business, we were the second-largest supplier of used Levi's 501 jeans in the world. Even though one LA-based competitor had more volume, we had better quality by far—thanks to the way we sourced our product.

My partners and I realized early on that purchasing from thrift shops would only make us dogs with chains around our necks. If we depended on a few thrift stores to supply us with 100 percent of our product, then some manager in a big, bodacious office could at any given time decide to cut off our supply by simply selling to one of our competitors. Like the U.S. with the dollar and Bitcoin, we knew we had to control the market. And that was exactly what we did.

We tried working with the thrift stores. Instead of putting their 501 jeans on the retail racks, they would ship them to a central location. We would even purchase jeans with holes. Pants that were in such poor shape that they would never, ever reach the retail floor accumulated in one single warehouse—thousands and thousands of Levi's 501 jeans piled up in a huge room. We would purchase the jeans and jackets every few weeks, spending hours sorting them into different price categories.

> **NOTE TO SELF**
> ### Betrayal = Opportunity
> Pay attention when you feel slighted or betrayed. Wherever they've taken advantage of your work is an opportunity to outwork and outsmart them.

Even though we taught thrift store staff all about how our business operated, they began to allow others to compete against us. We felt betrayed. But that betrayal also pointed us in the optimal direction.

To shore up our supply chain, we decided to skip the thrift stores and go directly to the public. We would advertise and pay cold, hard cash to the public for their used jeans.

This became a gigantic advantage of our business model. For one thing, it reversed our quality ratios. Now, 10,000 units produced 8,000 with no holes, with only the remaining 2,000 with holes and stains—the complete opposite of our prior thrift-store purchasing ratio. As our reclamation costs went down, it also solidified our brand as the best quality on the market. Our wholesale warehouse in southern Germany (and later in Spain) enjoyed a competitive advantage across the continent.

Eventually, the thrift stores asked us to return and start purchasing in bulk again. We did, but to our surprise they had allowed our competitors to only purchase the best jeans with no holes and no stains, leaving tens of thousands of jeans for the reclamation pile. This gave us negotiation leverage, ultimately forcing our competitors to take damaged and stained goods along with perfect pants on each order. We leveraged our huge market share in the used jeans business to negotiate from strength. Similar to how the planetary scale of the U.S. dollar is used by America to obtain desired results across the globe.

We focused on direct supply from the public. It took us a few years to set up a supply matrix that cascaded through the thirteen western states. To accomplish this, we would—for example—go to Topeka, Kansas, and advertise an upcoming event. We would rent space one weekend at the local mall, paying cash to the public for used jeans and jackets for that one weekend only. And it worked! We had lines of people with stacks of used jeans and jackets. We would put in fourteen hours a day buying what they brought us. And we did this all over the West.

Prices were as follows:

- Very dark blue, almost new jeans—$10
- Faded jeans with no holes—$7
- Jeans with up to three quarter-sized holes—$4
- Jeans with a few stains or large holes—$2
- Jeans with a crotch hole—$0.50

From there, we shipped the items to our warehouse in Salt Lake City, where seven full-time seamstresses made repairs. We put stained jeans through our steam machines and cleaned them with chemical methods. Some we washed, others we overdyed. From there, we sized, sorted, and arranged them for shipping with all of the proper notarized export and import documentation, utilizing low sales-tax rates for secondhand clothing. We could sell them as fast as we could ship them. The only slow months were July and August, as hot weather in Europe usually quashed denim sales.

To increase our supply chain matrix, prior to our weekend public events, we would visit as many pawn shops and consignment stores in the area as possible. We invited the principal owners to stop by the mall and observe exactly what we were doing. The reason: We wanted these brick-and-mortar establishments to continue pur-chasing from the public. We promised to coach their staff on how to grade and purchase correctly. We assured them that they would double their money each and every week. If they didn't achieve that, then we would offer additional training to their employees. To the pawnshop and consignment store owners, this was a double-margin product that moved off their inventory every single week. If they purchased $1,000 of product per week, then they should be able to sell it to our warehouse in Salt Lake City for $2,000 the next week.

Rolling that $1,000 could compound to $3,000 profit in about five weeks. Great return on investment (ROI).

After a big weekend, we would usually leave a city with ten to fifteen consignment stores or pawn shops set up to continue purchasing from the public. Every week thereafter, they'd be shipping loads and loads of product to our warehouse. Ultimately, we had a network of more than 650 locations buying from the public and filling our supply chain. This was in addition to the thrift stores' off-and-on supply. That helped us fulfill the varied demands of our market. Europe wanted the faded blue color, Japan wanted the very dark blue color, Spain wanted the overdye look, and some of them wanted an assortment with holes in the legs. Perfect . . . We had a lot of everything!

By this time both of my business partners were living in southern Germany, marketing and moving merchandise, and I was handling all sales to Asia. It was a fast, furious cash business. In addition to wholesale, my two partners ended up retailing our product by throwing weekend events at shopping malls in Eastern Europe. "Three days only! Original used American jeans!" We had obtained a fully internally integrated business model. We were "soup to nuts." We purchased from the public in America and sold to the public in Europe. We exploited the wave created by the United States and grew exponentially larger as we created our own luck. And it wasn't just in Europe.

Vintage denim was taking off in Japan. Teenagers in Tokyo were paying up to $6,000 for a dark-indigo-blue Levi's jacket with no holes and no stains made before 1945. Those price tags derived from Strauss's practice of using different indigo-blue ink and different styles and types of thread for each decade they produced the jackets. For instance, before the 1970s, the red company tag on the right back pocket or left chest pocket of a jacket had a capital "E" in the word—"LEVI'S." In the late 1970s the company changed that to a lower case "e." Japanese kids referred to the vintage ones as "Big Es"—old, collectible items that commanded premium prices in the high fashion stores of Tokyo.

> *"Definition of capitalism: Capitalism is when you come to a period and the next letter is much larger than all the other letters—that's capitalism."*
> —Unknown comedian from the Dry Bar

The indigo-blue dye used before 1950 is one reason the capital "E" or "Big E" became extremely popular. Accordingly, we trained our supply chains on the Big E market as hundreds of these vintage jeans and jackets flowed into our warehouse, mostly with holes and stains.

It didn't matter. Tokyo kids were determined to differentiate themselves from the other kids. In the United States, a high school kid gets a new sports car to stand out from the crowd. In Tokyo, rich kids have nowhere to park a car even if they could afford it. If they go to a party wearing Air Jordans? Big whoop. Several friends have the same shoes. But arrive wearing a Levi's first edition Big E jacket that was manufactured in 1942, with the old donut-style buttons, you were the coolest kid this side of the Ginza. It was hard to find someone with exactly the same jacket. As fashion magazines pushed this narrative, our warehouse in Salt Lake City was at the ready with hundreds of these items to sell each and every month.

And never lose sight that this entire business was all U.S. dollar–based: the dollar that the government continues to protect at every turn to this day. For an American entrepreneur using the U.S. dollar, could it get any better? Who in the world would fight this kind of wave? Ride it as far as it can take you.

Failure Is a Bitter Teacher

When I was fourteen years old, my fifteen-year-old cousin Bill received a new motorcycle for Christmas. After a few days, my uncle asked him, "Have you been riding?"

"Yes," replied my cousin.

"Have you wrecked yet?"

"No," said Bill, with pride in his safety record.

Then my uncle smirked. "Then you haven't been riding!"

I have always remembered this remark from my uncle; he made an everlasting impression on my young mind. Success is great, but failure can often teach us much more. Our Levi's story is certainly a great example of an incredibly successful venture. But they haven't all gone that way. One of my experiences in particular stands out to me—one where, unlike the wave we caught with Levi's, our timing was terrible.

By the mid-1990s, we knew that the used Levi's 501 jeans market would not last forever—fashion inevitably changes over time. Looking for opportunities to diversify our used clothing skills, we focused on the border of the United States and Mexico. We quickly identified a niche in the market. Six days a week, Mexican entrepreneurs crossed the border and purchased used American clothing for transport back into Mexico—a supply chain for thrift shops to our southern neighbor.

The business niche we identified focused on low product quality. The clothing that these wholesalers provided the Mexican entrepreneurs was thrift store leftovers. Basically, thrift stores in the United States would try to sell these products on their retail floors. After all the good stuff sold, the remaining items would be packed up and sent to the Mexican border for wholesale.

Our idea was to collect clothing from the U.S. public and send it directly to the border. In so doing, we'd offer superior quality and earn superior profits. That's because there would be no retail store to siphon off all the best items. The competition's stock was picked over before it even arrived. Our stock would still contain all of the best items. Provide the best-quality merchandise—it is a reliable market differentiator.

We met with a local charity and purchased custom-made steel containers. Next, we obtained permission to place them in supermarket parking lots. We negotiated a per-pound contract with the charity and put their name on the containers with the bold yellow lettering "Used Clothing Recycling Project." The public loved it! Helping a charity and recycling, all with the convenience of a drop-off in a parking lot they'd be at anyway! Great idea! Everybody wins! We thought it was pretty great ourselves, as our company would profit from clothing the public wanted to get rid of. Hmmm, making money from a steel dumpster—wonder where that idea came from?

We started accumulating so much clothing that we did not have anywhere to put it. The fire department visited our warehouse and saw mountains of clothing stacked to the roof. They gave us a warning to organize the merchandise fast or suffer a large fine. We moved quickly to lease a large warehouse on the border between Mexico and the United States. With hiring employees to run the operation, the planning, financing, contracts, and strategy took about fourteen months before the doors opened. In fact, it was already a pretty big

> **NOTE TO SELF**
> ## Keep an Eye on Politics
> Currency exchange rates and world politics can destroy a business that does not have its financial antennae up and extended. Always keep the radio frequency focused on the U.S. dollar.

operation prior to launch—new employees in multiple states, trucks, drivers, sorting employees, and insurance with payroll services and human resources policy manuals. But we experienced a harsh truth: timing can be your enemy as well as your friend.

We opened for business in November 1994. From day one, it was a super success. Our customer base exploded. We were profitable in only a few weeks. Hundreds of people started purchasing from our warehouse, ditching their prior suppliers and funneling their U.S. dollar purchasing power toward our company. The quality was fantastic, completely disrupting the local market. Our product was simply that much better. We kept up the pace, ordering more steel collection containers. We made inroad phone calls to additional supermarket chains as we ramped up for expansion and scale.

Then, within just seven weeks of our opening, with fourteen months of risk capital and sweat behind us, the Mexican peso was devalued in half—in one single day. Whatever the U.S. dollar economy had done, it forced a repricing of the peso. Short story, we closed the business. We negotiated out of our real estate and truck leases. We licked our newly formed financial wounds. It hurt—a lot.

We had done everything right. Identified a niche. Filled a problem with our business-minded, problem-solving selves. Identified our risks, mitigated them, and executed our business model. We were proud of our planning, strategy, and launch. It was a fantastic business model.

But what wasn't quite so fantastic was the possibility of currency fluctuations—a real possibility that we either forgot about or simply chose to ignore. It was a risk that smacked us down. We had better quality, a better supply chain, great employees—and terrible timing.

If we had launched it two years earlier, then maybe we could have weathered the currency storm. But even though we had filled a niche and addressed an opportunity, none of that matters when running a business. What matters is if you have the cash each Friday to pay your employees. If not, then look in the mirror and acknowledge it was a failure.

That is the life of an entrepreneur. Win, lose, but always try to learn from the experience. Even our jeans business came to an abrupt halt in early 1998. Three factors syncing up at the same time were the primary reasons:

- Teenagers in Europe didn't look at America's role in the Gulf War with fondness. From their perspective, the United States was bombing people in Kuwait for oil profits—nothing more.
- Second, the baggy pant look was taking the fashion world's attention away from tight-fitting 501 jeans. We fought back by selling 42-inch-waist 501s to the Japanese market, but the death spiral had begun.
- Third, particularly important to the focus of this book, the U.S. dollar had been weak for many years, helping U.S. companies export their products around the world. That was right where President Reagan wanted it, keeping Americans employed. But in 1997, the U.S. dollar got stronger and stronger. Our customers in Europe could not absorb the price increases due to currency exchanges.

We had caught the wave. But even the strongest wave won't last forever.

Want a Wave? Watch Your Timing

Since the U.S. dollar became a fiat currency in 1971, the world has transformed itself about every ten years. And each of those involved a wave, some of which I caught, others that I missed.

- **1989—The fall of the Soviet Union.** This was the wave we managed to catch with our blue jeans business.
- **1999—The dot.com bubble.** This is one I totally missed. I knew what was happening but never successfully leveraged it.
- **2008/2009—The Great Financial Crisis.** My partners and I nailed this one! We launched our third private equity fund in 2008, which purchased foreclosed properties that banks had on their balance sheets. As real estate was selling well below building costs as well as actual replacement dollar amounts, we pounced.
- **2019/2020—This one was a one-two punch.** The first was the existence of the lowest interest rates in recorded history. The second part was the COVID-19 pandemic. To take advantage, we launched real estate funds that assisted in the re-establishment and improvement of blighted geographical areas in the United States known as "opportunity zones" and established by the government. Anyone who invested in any one of these 8,764 specific geographic areas would receive tremendous tax advantages—a constant consideration for the would-be wealthy. Master the tax game because it is never going to go away.

A favorite joke of mine nicely summarizes the value of timing. Somewhere on an island very far away there's a smart man who climbs a banana tree. He picks a bushel of bananas and pitches them down to a guy on the ground who puts them in a big box. That box goes into a small truck. That truck delivers it to a big truck. The big truck transfers the box to a ship. That ship sails around the world to Los Angeles. The bananas are loaded on a big truck and delivered to a warehouse. Bananas are placed

on a small truck and arrive at my local supermarket. There I am on a Saturday afternoon looking at my beautiful yellow banana. Perfect. I buy it and take it home. The next morning, I wake up, come bouncing down the stairs, walk into the kitchen, and my banana—is completely brown.

Man . . . how do they do it? I mean . . . those guys are smart. The timing of that is almost unbelievable. I've told that joke many times over the years. And, if my timing is right when I deliver the punchline, I get a laugh every time. Again, timing is key. And that truth is only reinforced by the government's boxing in of Bitcoin.

Will the Fed introduce a digital dollar to further combat Bitcoin while strengthening the dollar itself? My bet is yes, using a well-thought-out and manufactured confluence of events. If your business antennae are extended, you will be able to see this wave coming and take advantage of it.

Similar to radio waves zooming past you 24/7, all that's needed is a good antenna to listen in. Even with all the government has done and will continue to do to protect its number one product—however you may feel about all that—America is the greatest country in the world for entrepreneurs. If you are an entrepreneur, then the day you moved to the U.S.A. is the day you won the lottery. If you were born in the U.S.A. and you want to be your own boss someday, then your birthday was your winning lottery day. No matter who you are, don't waste your lottery ticket. Keep your antennae up. And don't fight the wave, ride it. It may take you further than you could possibly imagine.

BOXING IN BASICS

6A. Keep your eyes open for opportunity and know what to do when you spot it—as I did in a steel dumpster filled with used blue jeans. Your intuition will pipe up when you're being guided to the best possible opportunities.

6B. Controlling the market is everything when you want to box in your opponent. In our case, we boxed others in by controlling supply as often as possible.

6C. Boxing in an opponent can also be achieved through better quality—as was the case with our jeans. Regularly consider how you can provide a better-quality product or service than your competitor and know that this needs to be considered at regular intervals throughout your entire business career. Spend the time and exert the effort to have a great product.

6D. Timing can prove to be a wild card. In our case, we had a great idea and lousy timing. To catch a wave and ride it, timing is critical. With entrepreneurship comes inherent risk, so accept that sometimes you just won't know when timing will be on your side, but you need to continue to move forward with your good ideas either way.

6E. There's no other country in the world that affords better opportunities for boxing in personal success than the United States. All you need are antennae extended up to pick up on waves that afford enormous opportunities.

CHAPTER 7
Negotiation

Negotiation is not about striking a fair deal. It's about discovering the limits of what the opposing party will agree to. Negotiation is *discovery*.

In a wartime prison swap, one prisoner for one prisoner seems like a fairly negotiated deal. But that's not the job of a negotiator. A negotiator's assignment is to discover if the other side would trade one prisoner plus his wife and one child in exchange for a single soldier. Three people for one. This is the task of a great negotiator—discovering just how far the other side is willing to go using multiple tactics, such as bluffing and delayed response. Pushing the other side to the brink of walking away from the negotiation table allows a negotiator to complete their assigned task. A small child can negotiate a one-for-one swap. Easy! But discovering what the opposing party will surrender in their quest to obtain what you possess is the goal. Leveraging everything, with tactical maneuvering to learn the limits of their compromise. That's the skill set of a great negotiator.

And, like the U.S. government is seeking to do to Bitcoin, gold, China's yuan and all other competitors, effective negotiation is all about boxing in your opponent by boxing in probabilities—what can you do to control them while limiting their options to fight back?

Repeat Their Demands, Then Ask One Question

Here's one of a skilled negotiator's best tactics. Repeating what their opponent wants them to do, they simply tack on the question: "How can I do that?" They then promptly shut their mouths and allow their opponent to uncomfortably discover all the obstacles to comply with their demands. The negotiator is effectively allowing the opposing party to argue their side. Processing each issue one by one, they come to understand all the reasons that prevent anyone from complying with their ultimatums.

Here's a hypothetical example, involving a rudimentary negotiation pattern that I believe has been going on for years between Saudi Arabia and the United States.

Saudi Prince: "Mr. President, our two countries have a long history together. But the time has come to allow China to purchase oil from Saudi Arabia in its own currency, abandoning the U.S. dollar requirement. China is a very large customer; therefore, we must make this change."

U.S. President: "I agree. Our countries have a very long history and close partnership. We deploy our navy at great expense to protect your shipping lanes and your borders. Evil people all over the world are deterred from attacking a Saudi shipment, as they will then deal with the united front of the U.S. Armed Forces. Additionally, we provide you with state-of-the-art fighter jets and ongoing training with thousands of U.S. personnel stationed inside your country. We value your friendship and your support of the U.S. dollar in all petroleum transactions across the globe. If Saudi

Arabia removes itself from the petrodollar, how will I, as the U.S. president, be able to convince the United States Congress to continue this worldwide security and military support for your country? Can you explain to me how I am supposed to do that?"

Then the U.S. president stops talking, allowing the Saudi prince to attempt to answer this question. The key here is that the negotiator needs to stop talking—then keep quiet. Let your opponent tangle themselves into a knot and eventually begin to make your case for you.

Correctly articulating and repeating back your opponent's proposal demonstrates the understanding of their position. This brilliant negotiation maneuver forces capitulation. One by one, your opponent solves your issues. Challenging them with, "Is that what you really want?" and "How can I achieve that?"—puts the ball in the opposite court.

This strategy can also be subliminally executed in small, subset conversations during an entire negotiation process. This prompts your opponent to devote time and thought to understanding your problems. Repeat their demands, then ask: "How can I do that?"

This may not work for the U.S., as Saudi Arabia might decide to ditch the dollar. But the U.S. will make it as painful as possible or offer a carrot (i.e., help them develop a nuclear program).

The Golden Phrase

I was thirty years old when I first thought of the Golden Phrase. It bubbled up in my mind out of necessity. I was continually losing in conversational battles with older, wealthier, and more experienced people. I had to figure out a way to win. Thus, my Golden Phrase in negotiation manifested in my mind at the perfect moment.

People entering into a business deal with large monetary potential must execute an agreement. And many times, this agreement is not written but just a handshake. Often a younger person—me (before I was thirty years old)—is seeking a business relationship with an older and much more financially successful businessperson. This sometimes happens with family members, such as a rich uncle or aunt. Both parties are trying to agree on how and who gets to share in the profits. The younger person respects the older person and does not want to offend them during the early stages of the relationship.

What often happens is, after discussing the terms, the older person will offer their hand and say, "Let's shake on it." The younger person, not wanting to offend, says, "Shouldn't we write this down?" The older person quickly replies: "Don't you trust me?"

And there is the dilemma. Not shaking on it may offend the other person, killing the deal entirely. The younger person cannot risk pushing the issue for a written contract. It sends a message implying lack of trust, potentially leaving the younger person with no deal, empty-handed.

This is a dilemma of many would-be entrepreneurs, one I dealt with many times.

Sometimes the older person will draft a loosely written one- or two-page document that does not say much and avoids many important points of the business relationship—which, of course, are all central to the younger person's interests. The younger person pushes for more pages, more paragraphs with details. Then a bit of deal fatigue clouds the discussion. The older, more financially established person usually says, "Look, we cannot possibly write down every little detail. It will take too long; at some point we just have to trust each other." And the dilemma arises again. Does the younger person keep pushing? Or is it smarter to just accept a weakly drafted agreement, out of fear of offending the other side?

What often emerges is a flimsy agreement, signed between a rich aunt and her very talented, ambitious niece or nephew, for example. Family business agreements rarely have any written agreements—or at best they consist of a two-paragraph signed document. To state it plainly and for the avoidance of doubt: this is a huge mistake.

But there's a solution, a phrase that occurred to me many years ago—one that will not offend and allows for a solid written agreement, even with close family members (those most likely to be taken back by a perceived "lack of trust"). It's simple, to the point, and honest. It is golden (meaning it will save you a lot of gold over time). I taught my children this phrase when they were young. Not only has it worked 100 percent of the time, but I have also tried imagining a scenario where it would not work. And I do not believe any exists.

Here it is. When your rich Aunt Betty asks, "Don't you trust me?" your reply should be as follows:

"Oh, yes, Aunt Betty! I trust you completely, that is why I am entering into this business arrangement with you, but I don't trust your children's attorney."

You've just put your opponent in checkmate. There is no comeback, no rejoinder. Aunt Betty has no countermoves to this maneuver. There is only reality. Because it's an undeniable fact.

Scan the QR code to watch the author discuss
the Golden Phrase in negotiation.

Let's continue the discussion with Aunt Betty.

"Aunt Betty, if this business arrangement goes as planned and we start making a lot of money, what happens if, God forbid, you die in a freak car accident? I won't be dealing with you anymore. I will be dealing with your children's lawyer as your estate is being worked out. And that attorney's job is to protect your children's assets. This attorney is going to look at me and say, 'If you and Aunt Betty had a financial arrangement, why didn't you write it down? As an attorney for the children's estate, it is impossible for me to negotiate a verbal contract. A contract that supposedly was agreed upon between the two of you.' Aunt Betty, this is the attorney that I don't trust. That is why we need an agreement, written down, that includes all of the small and large details."

Personal details may vary between situations, but this approach will work in those as well.

If Aunt Betty has no children: "Aunt Betty, I do not trust your spouse's lawyer."

If Aunt Betty is not married: "Aunt Betty, I do not trust your estate attorney."

It truly is the Golden Phrase.

You've effectively boxed in your opponent in negotiation—just as the United States is attempting to box in Bitcoin and the yuan, etc., for the outcome of protecting its number one product—the U.S. dollar.

The Junkyard Dog Negotiation—Compared to What?

Taking a quick glance down a wooded path, there are two very large piercing eyes locked onto your position. This large Russian wolf has been tracking you for the past six minutes. The crisp air and the pulsating human breath continually surrender your position to this apex predator. Your mortality status is now aggressively compromised. Question: If you had a choice, would you want (a) your golden lab retriever by your side or (b) the meanest junkyard dog on a thick chain snarling like a starving lion? Which would you choose?

The junkyard dog is so cocky it has no hesitation in taking on a wolf. Warning! This dog is so vicious that it will sometimes bite you, even though you are the human who feeds it. That's the type of dog that can take on a wolf. This dog does so by making the wolf think twice, or better yet, by taking the wolf out completely.

You don't like this dog, but the real question is: You don't like the dog compared to what? Compared to being eaten by a wolf? You don't like the junkyard dog that sometimes bites you and that is now the best friend you've got?

This principle works the same in challenges humans are required to confront. It's common knowledge that humble, great jet fighter pilots do not exist. To be a great jet fighter pilot, humility is not at the top of the qualification list. There's no "Aw, shucks" in their working vocabulary. The cocky fighter pilot is the only pilot who has a chance of success. You might not like their cocky attitude, but compared to what? When a very difficult job requires execution, a self-indulgent junkyard dog or incredibly cocky fighter pilot is the ticket. When fighting off wolves, humility is not a desirable attribute.

The point is, there are some tasks, assignments, and jobs that can only be accomplished by a mean junkyard dog. Even though you may have to endure stitches on your hand from gashing-teeth marks, those doctor visits are far less gruesome than being eaten by a wolf in the forest. Again, when complaining about anything, the question must be asked: Compared to what?

The brilliant real estate mogul and famous podcaster Jason Hartman coined the phrase "Compared to what?" Translated: All moaning and complaining become pointless without asking the question, "Compared to what?"

Granted, a junkyard dog doesn't offer an optimal relationship. But he's not built to be a friendly dog that can play nicely with your small children while being mean enough to take down a wolf. (That dog does not exist.)

British Bulldog

Just to reinforce the point, here's an example from history of a junkyard dog in action on a grand scale. The year is 1940, the German Nazi army has invaded France after breaking the Maginot Line, and France's ally, the British Empire, is maneuvering its mighty naval fleet around Europe to mitigate and eventually stop the German advancement. Understand—Britain and France are allies, and the U.S. had not yet entered WWII.

The British were convinced that a fleet of French warships was about to fall into German hands. These ships would then be repurposed and used to fight the British Navy. England insisted that these French ships be turned over and rerouted to English ports to join Britain's fleet. The French argued and then refused.

So, the British Navy fired on the French ships and sank them, thwarting Germany's plan to seize them. *Whaaaaatttt? They are their allies—aren't they?!* you may be wondering. Once again, the junkyard dog is so mean that sometimes it bites you.

The French might have done well to ask themselves: *Comparé à quoi?* (Compared to what?) Would they have rather had the Nazis overrun their country or lose a few warships? They might not have liked either choice, but with a junkyard dog, that isn't a part of the question. You can only choose between two scenarios.

In 1941 in the wake of Pearl Harbor, the United States entered World War II. The next year Lieutenant General Dwight D. Eisenhower (a U.S. president in the making) moved his base of operation from London to Gibraltar. He did this to be closer to the planned invasion of North Africa. General Eisenhower had been warned that the French Navy might put up a fight against British troops and their naval landing in North Africa. *What? Why?* Why would the French want to impede the British (and American troops) from pushing the Germans out of Africa? One reason was the supreme Vichy commander, French Admiral Jean Darlan, had never forgiven the abrupt British attack on his French warships in 1940. A thirst for revenge that needed to be quenched.

Admiral Darlan finally agreed to a ceasefire with the British and came to an agreement with General Eisenhower, allowing his continued military operations in Morocco and Algeria.

However, on December 24 an assassin shot and killed French Admiral Darlan in Algiers. His assassin was an anti-Vichy volunteer who was training as a French commando. Evidently loyal to his country, he did not care for Darlan's backing down to the British after what they had done to the French Navy.

> **NOTE TO SELF**
> **Vote for the Junkyard Dogs**
>
> Always vote for politicians who have the audacity to defeat wolves (example: China and Russia), thus enabling my family the continued right of life, liberty, and the pursuit of happiness under the U.S. Constitution.

Ultimately, the British were a major part of the victory against the Axis powers. France was eventually liberated from German occupation. Junkyard dogs that are mean enough to kill a wolf are arrogant enough to take a piece of flesh out of your leg.

When you say you don't like something, you need to follow up with the question: Compared to what? Would you rather have the Nazi party occupying Paris or lose a fleet of French warships? Well, I don't like either choice! That is the point of the junkyard dog. You can't have what you want—you can only choose between two scenarios, however flawed.

I don't like the Fed's printing of trillions of dollars and controlling global trade with their world reserve currency. Many don't like it, but what is the alternative? And are gold bugs or devoted Bitcoin neophytes going to try to kill the U.S. dollar? Infighting like the murder of French Admiral Darlan by his own soldier?

The U.S. dollar may well be the largest Ponzi scheme ever. Monopoly and Ponzi wrapped up in one package. But there is no mathematical way to taper a large Ponzi scheme. The only way out is to play it to the end. I did not create this Ponzi scheme; I was born into it. If the U.S. dollar is worthless tomorrow morning, then my parents' retirement is gone. My children's wealth has vanished. And they would all have to move into my basement. But wait, I would be broke, also! Therefore, I am aligned with the Fed to support and promote the U.S. dollar . . . because the alternative is even worse.

The examples from World War II underscore what an unknown author said about history that I have cited previously: "There are only two productive things someone can do with history—learn from it or forgive." As the Spaniard Inigo Montoya says in the movie *The Princess Bride*, "There is not a lot of money in revenge." And smart entrepreneurs refuse to use their precious brainpower on unproductive activities.

Attrition Has a High Win Rate

One obvious but no less salient lesson from the promotion and protection of the world's number one product is to learn from those who consistently succeed. For me, figuring out how someone becomes best in class and how they negotiated themselves through many impossible situations is always the most interesting part of history. I usually don't focus on who won a battle or became the top dog of some industry. I'm more fascinated by *how* they did what they did. I want to know the story between the beginning and the achievement.

The "who did that" is trivial to me, but the "how" is captivating. *How* did they prepare and position themselves to increase the odds of success, particularly when the odds were utterly stacked against them? *How* did they stay nimble and adjust and execute a plan consistently, day in and day out?

Usually, it's because they continuously box in their probabilities. They employ the same strategy that the Fed is using against Bitcoin, the yuan, and gold. Successful people build a personal plan to succeed and execute their campaign every day to box in their success. Boxing in their business. Not allowing it to fail. And that goes for some unconventional role models.

When I was in my teenage years and early twenties, I did not understand—nor did I like—Muhammad Ali. But now, with a lot of grey hair on my head, I have become a fan. I now understand his brilliance and have come to appreciate the challenges and issues that he had to deal with. His strategy of negotiating and positioning to become a winner on many different levels is a study in greatness.

Ali's first shot at the heavyweight championship was against the formidable Sonny Liston—who was regarded as unbeatable, as his punching power and size were intimidating for any challenger. But Ali—then known as Cassius Clay—started to box him in before they even stepped into the ring. In a departure from staid tradition, Ali almost got into a fistfight with Liston during the weigh-in. He shouted insults about Liston's character. He was abrasive and demeaning: "If you want to lose your money, then bet on Sonny!"

It was a perfect box-in. When Liston entered the ring against Clay, he was bent on revenge—where, as has been said, there's not a lot of money. Clay beat Liston. Liston, believing it was a fluke, scheduled a rematch, and Ali once again worked his inflammatory rhetoric to pierce Sonny's confidence. This time, it took a mere one minute, forty-nine seconds—an outcome which Ali announced later that he carefully avoided predicting: "If I said I would knock out Sonny Liston in one minute and forty-nine seconds of the first round, that would have hurt the gate."

Liston was by no means the only victim of Ali's brilliance at getting under an opponent's skin. Fighting against George Foreman—a blistering boxer with enormous size and power—an overweight Ali appeared utterly overmatched. But, again, he boxed in his opponent, this time in the ring and using physical as well as psychological strategy.

For much of the fight, Ali would purposely place his back against the ropes and stand there, talking smack to Foreman. He allowed the larger, stronger fighter to punch and punch some more—the famous "Rope a Dope" strategy, which, when you think about it, carries a double meaning. Time and time again as each round started, Ali would walk out to the center of the ring and immediately take a few steps backward and put his back against the ropes—then cover up, talk more smack, endure a barrage of punches, then talk more smack, shouting his "disappointment" that Foreman couldn't punch harder than that.

On points, Ali was losing round after round. But he was exhausting Foreman while conserving his own energy—that is, until the eighth round. As Foreman slowed down, Ali picked a small window of opportunity and came off the ropes, landing a few precisely calculated punches. Foreman dropped to the canvas and stayed there for a count of ten.

Not only is Ali's story an iconic example of boxing in your opponent, but it's also an example of method within seeming madness. I ask my friends: "If you and I were sent back in time to be Muhammad Ali's counselors and mentors, we would probably, like almost everyone else at the time, tell him to tamp down his style. 'Don't goad the opponent.' 'Be a statesman and let your fists do the talking in the ring.' In other words, 'Be conventional.'"

And we couldn't have been more misguided. Ali was an unconventional strategist who knew how to win. He used his rhetoric to get inside the heads of all his opponents—not just the opponent who was directly in front of him but also opponents he would face in the future. It was a continuous negotiation, an ongoing dance.

Additionally, it was also clear that Ali—as I mentioned earlier—was also a constant student of the "how." As he once said: "A man who views the world the same at fifty as he did at twenty has wasted thirty years of his life."

To George Foreman's credit and not thinking like his younger self, he returned to the sport of boxing at the age of forty-five years old and regained the heavyweight championship belt. *A forty-five-year-old?* Wow, he really did reinvent himself.

Can a Good Journal Be a Negotiating Tool?

In the mid-1990s I had a good friend named Samantha. She was an incredibly talented person. Through a few very strategic moves, she became chief of operations in a small public company with about 150 employees. And to my amazement, she had also obtained almost 4 percent of the stock in the company. Still, even with her equity position, she was not a member of the board.

After about two years in this position, the company's domestic marketing and sales division began to crumble. One of the company's longtime third-party marketing firms decided to go out on their own and directly compete, poaching employees away.

Company revenue continued to decline, and the investment banking firm that was responsible for taking the company public was in the office a lot, screaming at the company's vice president and president in closed conference rooms. But the employees could hear what was going on halfway through the building.

After several months of this continued bashing by the investment bankers, Samantha's antennae told her that a big lawsuit was in the works. The investment bankers were going to drag everyone to court for years and years. Samantha could see they were on a collision course.

She was right in the middle. In trying to keep the company afloat, she had to do her job and support the CEO/president. But she couldn't tick off the investment bankers when they called on the phone to ask questions about the internal conditions of the company. Over time, she realized they were going to need a scapegoat to divert attention from themselves. They were going to tell their investors about *someone* who messed everything up, who didn't follow their directions, and who eventually lost their investment dollars: her.

She wasn't going to allow this to happen. She was not going to get boxed in, like Bitcoin.

Her strategy? Keep a journal. Not only did she maintain a detailed record of daily events—filled with wire transfer details, odd payroll checks, irregular financial moves, dates of corporate meetings, and a record of strange decision-making—but she also made sure to mail a copy of that day's journal to herself each night as she passed the post office box. When the letter arrived at her house a few days later, she did not open it. She put it in a filing box with all the other letters, using the postage date stamp as proof of when the journal entry was made.

> **NOTE TO SELF**
> ## Keep Your Records Straight
> Confirming verbal agreements with the written word keeps you from getting boxed in. A good journal can be mightier than the sword.

She had theorized that a good attorney would first question the authenticity of the dates of some of the journal entries. So, in effect, she used the U.S. Postal Service to time-stamp her journal. How brilliant is that?

There was more. Samantha wrote her mailing address on the back side of the envelope—the side that closes and seals the envelope—and made sure the address overlapped the seal itself. That would prevent anyone from trying to open the envelope, changing the contents, and then resealing the envelope. It would just be too obvious that the letter had been tampered with. Samantha was using the Fed's Bitcoin strategy. Box your opponent in, slowly and methodically. Brilliant.

As expected, the company continued to decline. Samantha resigned and moved on. Sure enough, about a year and half later attorneys for both sides—the investment bankers and the president of the publicly held company—subpoenaed Samantha for a court deposition. On the plane ride there, she reviewed her second copy of the journal entries. The hundreds of stamped envelopes were safely in her travel bag, under lock and key.

As luck would have it, when she arrived the schedule had been adjusted. As a result, she had time to speak to lawyers for both parties in separate, private conversations. In both discussions, she explained how her deposition would proceed. In response to a question, she said, "I'm going to thumb through these envelopes that I have. I'm going to ask each lawyer to view the envelope to decide if the envelope looks tampered with in any way." She would then request that their statements be put into the deposition record. Then she would open the envelope that was relevant to the question asked, and she would read the contents of the journal entry. The whole process exuded integrity.

One of the lawyers chuckled a little bit and praised her journaling with a decided air of condescension. That didn't last; clearly, he hadn't been paying attention. When Samantha showed him the stack of envelopes and how she had written the addresses, then and only then did the attorney notice that the U.S. Postal Service stamped dates were intact. He gulped loudly enough for everyone in the room to hear. Then Samantha smashed the final nail into the coffin that housed the attorneys' scheme.

"I read the second copy of all these journal entries on the plane ride down here today," she said matter-of-factly, "and, to tell you the truth, looking back on it, I seriously cannot tell you who the bad guys or good guys are. That will be your job after my deposition is finished."

Samantha was excused to go sit out in the lobby as each attorney seized a phone to discuss the situation. One of the lawyers actually asked if he could have a copy of the second copy of the journal. Suppressing the desire to return the patronizing chuckle she had received just a few minutes before, she said, "Of course not." If they wanted to know the content of the journals, they would have to depose her under oath with a court recorder. Just like they were bound by law to do.

After an hour, one of the attorneys came out and told Samantha that the deposition had now been rescheduled again. She went back to the airport, flew home, and, to this day has never heard from anyone on this subject again. Samantha told me that she still has those envelopes in a box somewhere.

Just like the Fed is trying to put Bitcoin in a box, Samantha knew to control the outcome, control adversaries, and control the game. She became a junkyard dog who even the most aggressive wolf would shy away from.

Samantha told me that the strategy was so good that it still would have worked if the stamped envelopes had nothing in them. I looked at her, she looked at me, and we just laughed. Strategy, negotiation, intimidation, attrition, and even bluffing are all skills—part of boxing in the probabilities of success, and they should be food for thought for every leader and business owner.

When Negotiating, It's Team, Team, Team

A central element to the success of Boxing In Bitcoin, the yuan, or gold is that, whether by choice or force, everybody with a stake in the U.S. dollar is very much on the same team. That team includes the U.S. president, the IRS, the SEC, the U.S. Navy, the Fed, and you and me. We are all on the same team. This is important because there are more threats to the U.S. dollar than just Bitcoin (if, given its position, you can genuinely call it a serious threat, at least for now).

China is currently seeking to create a second world currency to compete against the U.S. dollar. It is nicknamed the "BRICS Dollar," representing Brazil, Russia, India, China, and South Africa. On the drawing board for several years, it's backed by commodities such as oil, wheat, and gold. They are putting their team together with additional members—Saudi Arabia, Iran, Ethiopia, Argentina, and the United Arab Emirates. Are they aligned enough to launch this new BRICS dollar? Time will tell.

And it appears they have their own junkyard dog—Russia. If the BRICS dollar is designed to be 100 percent backed by commodities, it makes sense why Russia invaded Ukraine for its massive amounts of grain and oil. The war is a primitive, junkyard-dog-like move to acquire more hard commodities before the launch of the BRICS dollar. Frankly, if I were the president of one of these BRICS countries, I probably would employ the same strategy.

The vast majority of my wealth and yours is in the U.S. dollar. Therefore, I support the U.S. dollar. And not just for selfish reasons. I support it because of the positive worldwide effects it produced after the Bretton Woods Agreement. Since 1944, nations around the world have, for the first time in history, been able to sell their goods and services to other countries with no fear. Since 1944 more people have been lifted out of poverty at a faster rate than at any time in world history. Go ahead, bash the U.S. dollar and the U.S. military all you like, but world poverty has greatly declined through the means of a stable currency backed by safe seabound transportation.

Now, I admit, this situation is not optimal—but compared to what? That's why I'm on this team. A team with a vicious junkyard dog (the Fed) on its side. Boxing In Bitcoin and fighting off other aggressors is a team sport—an ongoing negotiation, a never-ending dance. The more people and muscle you have on your side, the greater your strength.

We were all born into a Ponzi scheme—the U.S. dollar. Not a perfect system, but again, compared to what? There is no alternative except to push the game as far as it can go. I didn't create it, but I am in it. Plus, I have a junkyard dog on my side to fight off the wolves. Team, team, team.

> NOTE TO SELF
> ### Don't Go It Alone
> For the U.S. dollar to rise to number one status, it required a team effort. Why would your supersized business idea warrant anything less?

Bluffing as a Negotiation Tool

In November 2022, the Fed announced the testing of its own U.S. digital dollar with the help of Wells Fargo and Citibank. Then a few months later in March 2023, the Fed shut down the top three cryptocurrency banks in the United States—Silvergate Bank, Silicon Valley Bank, and Signature Bank. Coincidence? These two moves in concert were a signal, a bluff to all banks: "If you are not on the U.S. digital dollar bandwagon, beware!" The Fed has no intention of shutting down hundreds of regional banks. But do the executives at these current regional banks know that?

Bluffing has always been a mainstay of the back-and-forth dance between the Fed and Bitcoin. To cite just one ongoing example, Bitcoin backers have argued that much of Fed Chairman Jerome Powell's aggressive comments about Bitcoin amount to little more than a bluff designed to tamp down interest in cryptocurrency. It's possible. If bluffing is a go-to strategy in Boxing In Bitcoin, it should be a part of your business strategy as well. One effective way to dislodge a bluff is to use the burn-off strategy.

The Burn-Off

Let's start with what I call the "burn-off negotiation strategy," using two examples. Deadlocks and impasses are common in negotiation. Both parties are at deal fatigue, and neither one will budge. Using a burn-off clause can reignite productive negotiation. The key is to accurately depict future changes in each party's perspective.

Here's how you can use burn-off in a loan negotiation:

Your team is acquiring a very large real estate portfolio of 5,000 storage units. To obtain necessary financing, the bank is requiring that every team member provide a personal guarantee for the thirty-year mortgage. Being a guarantor for thirty years would hinder your team's ability to obtain financing on additional loans, both business and personal. Your team refuses, and the bank refuses to issue the loan. The negotiation is stuck.

Then your team offers a burn-off solution. To mitigate the bank's risk, the owners will sign personal guarantees. However, when twenty-four months of successful on-time payments occur, the personal guarantee will be reduced in half. Further, at thirty-six months, the guarantees are eliminated completely. This works because the bank's risk is reduced over time, and a history of reliable payments further ensures the safety of the loan. The personal guarantees are "burned off."

The second example that follows employs a burn-off in a prenuptial agreement.

A successful businessman goes through a nasty divorce, and his wife ends up with the lion's share of their assets. Since then, he has built and sold a second business and recently retired. But love has found him once again. The new fiancée is also previously divorced and has a prestigious career that will allow her to retire in about twelve years.

He wants her to sign a prenuptial agreement and then travel the world with him. From her perspective, if this second marriage ends in divorce, she would have a very difficult time reentering the workforce at her current senior position and still retiring in twelve years. This prenuptial agreement carries too much risk for her if something goes wrong. They love each other, but they're at a stalemate.

Enter a burn-off. One possibility is a ten-year schedule. If either party files for divorce in the first year of marriage, then both parties agree that the man's estate will pay $100,000 to the woman. If either files for divorce in the second year of marriage, she would then receive $200,000, then $300,000 in the third year, and $400,000 in the fourth year up until ten years—a $1 million payout at that point. If the couple is married ten years and one day, the prenuptial agreement is burned off and no longer is in effect.

The man might argue that if he dies after ten years, the woman would receive all of his wealth, with none left for his children and grandchildren. This can be remedied by the man distributing his inheritance to his children prior to the ten-year mark or by obtaining life insurance policies that would benefit either his children or wife.

A burn-off strategy allows negotiations to continue. It dislodges many impasses and mitigates the risks for both parties. I have seen it work several times, with both second marriages and bank loans. Some might think burn-off scenarios aren't fair or equitable, but that is not their purpose. A burn-off strategy is designed to find out what the opposing party can or cannot live with. And in the end, that is exactly what negotiation is all about. Negotiation is **not** about striking a fair deal; it's about discovering the limits of what the opposing party will agree to.

The U.S. dollar team has employed all the negotiation tools discussed in this chapter consistently and with great success, as well as various derivative strategies. Learn from them and watch as your negotiation skills blossom. And, just to be thorough, these powerful negotiation skills can also prove very handy around the house. Just ask my wife.

A few years ago, when I learned about the extremely low taxes in Puerto Rico, I did all the research and was ready to pull the trigger. We would purchase a home in Puerto Rico and physically be off the mainland for at least 180 days per year. If we could accomplish this, our yearly tax bill could be as low as 4 percent. Only pay 4 percent in taxes each year and still live in a territory of the United States. What a bargain!

Now, listen to how my wife took to this idea as she contemplated being away from her grandkids for 180 days a year. Pay attention to how concise and succinct my wife's dialogue was to convince me to not move to Puerto Rico. And please remember, I consider myself a pretty good negotiator:

She: "Let me get this straight. We are wealthy?"

Me: "Yes."

She: "And that means we can live anywhere we want?"

Me: "Yes, that is correct."

She: "So, remind me again, what is the reason we have to move to Puerto Rico?"

Me: "Because we are wealthy."

She: *Moving in close, giving me a small kiss, pulling her head back slightly, pausing, and gazing into my eyes, my wife says with a smile—*"**Checkmate.**"

She had boxed me in. The negotiation was over before it began.

BOXING IN BASICS

7A.   Repeat their request and ask: "How can I do that?"

7B.   Use the Golden Phrase in negotiation: "I trust you; I just don't trust your children's attorney."

7C.   Employ the junkyard dog negotiation: get a dog so mean, sometimes it bites you.

7D.   Use the rope-a-dope strategy and attrition to tire out your opponent.

7E.   Box in your luck; don't give it too many paths to escape.

7F.   Decide what team you are on and when you feel like complaining, ask yourself: Compared to what?

7G.   Keep a journal with detailed notes and verified dates.

7H.   A burn-off strategy can end deadlocks and mitigate risks in situations like loans and prenuptials.

CHAPTER 8
Team of Success

Go BIG.

I was forty years old, and it was time to go BIG. No more small, medium, or even relatively large ideas. I was ready to shoot for the moon and go for it. Starting and co-founding businesses was my mantra. I had done so fourteen times up until this point—three ideas lost money, and three made me a lot of money. The rest did well and offered good experience.

By forty years old, I had played my life's chessboard out, using probabilities and timelines. After many months of mentally mapping out my future business plans, there were two probabilities:

- **Scenario #1.** If I waited until I was fifty years old to go BIG and risk everything to start a supersized business idea, then I would not know if it was going to fail until I was fifty-six years old. It would require about six years to really work the idea from every angle, from every perspective, and from every business model before I would give up. Sure, small companies and small ideas do not take six years to really work all the kinks out, but a supersized idea may take that long. Amazon lost money for almost a decade before it became profitable. Therefore, I thought, if I lost all that time and money at fifty-six, then I would need a few years to recover and get back on my feet financially. This timetable would barely allow me to retire at age seventy.

- **Scenario #2.** If I went BIG at forty, risked everything, and failed by forty-six, then I would have plenty of time to recover financially and retire comfortably by sixty. The obvious conclusion for me: I had to go BIG at forty or not go at all, because at fifty the risk would be too great. At that late stage in my life, the logical mind would hinder my capacity for risk so close to retirement age. That may not be true for you, but it was for me.

Age forty was a window in time that I had to jump through or possibly miss the opportunity forever. If I didn't go for it now, I might never have another chance. Shooting for the stars is a dangerous game. But this game needs to be played at least once in a person's lifetime. So, I jumped.

I needed to study the greatest product of all time—how it became so dominant—and, from there, implement similar strategies for my personal greatest product: that product being *me*. Nothing in this universe can produce more success for me than myself. Therefore, I decided that I am my greatest product, just like the U.S. dollar is America's greatest product. And duplicating myself, or better said, scaling my businesses, was an essential part of the plan.

It's important to note that we can observe circumstances like the boxing in of Bitcoin from several angles. Mostly, we've discussed how to observe these larger trends and strategize for professional and financial gain, but we can also observe with the intent to improve ourselves as individuals—in this case, I picked up on the fact that to be truly successful, I couldn't only rely on myself.

Like the U.S. government bringing on brilliant team members like JPMorgan to box in an opponent, I knew from the outset that additional skill sets needed to be acquired by building a team.

First, I Did the Math

When I tell people that I am a co-founder of a $28 billion family of private equity funds, they often have difficulty comprehending the magnitude of those words. In fact, as I write this, it is still difficult for *me* to believe, even though I was there every step of the way witnessing the incredible sixteen-year growth of a supersized business model. Grasping the number one billion was difficult—until I did the math.

Here's an exercise to illustrate that. Start counting to one billion right now, saying each number out loud—"one, two, three, four"—every second and continuing without sleeping or eating or taking a restroom break. How long would it take to count to one billion seconds?

a.   31.7 hours
b.   31.7 days
c.   31.7 months
d.   31.7 years

The correct answer is that 31.7 years equals one billion seconds. And, with me, it looked as though I would need all the time I could possibly get. I have never liked being told what to do, an attitude that made me, shall we say, a "reluctant" employee. I had to be my own boss. With this inherent arrogance, there was no other logical course of action that would enable my success. Working for other people, building their dream instead of mine, was exhausting to even think about. For me, running my own business wasn't just a goal. It was the only probable path to success. Given my personality, any other route would likely lead to failure.

In 1988, I had many advantages. I was healthy and strong and—needless to say—very motivated. On the other hand, I had been a poor student, was an extremely slow reader, and had no mentors or money and no applicable business experience when I graduated college. Some years ago, the United States also formulated a plan to be the boss. To control its future by developing a team to create and support the most successful product of all time. And its power has increased over time, just like mine has.

Still, I lived in the United States of America—the most fertile place in the world for would-be entrepreneurs. This was the place to dream and dream big—and I did. When I began dreaming of success, I often thought about Mr. Sam Walton, the founder of Walmart. When he was about to stop working, he proposed a retirement package for himself. He asked the board of directors for $1 a day from each Walmart store around the world. At the time, a Walmart store's average size was more than 30,000 square feet of retail space with thousands of items on the shelves. All Sam Walton wanted was $1 a day per store. It seemed both incredible—and a little crazy.

But it wasn't so crazy. For one thing, Sam had a net worth in the billions—the money didn't really mean anything to him. For another, do the math. Walmart had some 5,000 stores at Sam's retirement—5,000 stores, $1 a day multiplied by 30 days came to a $150,000 monthly retirement check. Most of us could be rather happy living on $150,000 a month when retired. Just living on the dividends, not selling assets. What a goal! And the fertile business landscape of America can make it all happen. Walmart's story resonated in my young but aspiring soul. It was difficult to comprehend at the time, but strangely I believed it was possible. Finding real-life examples like that pushed me to expand my own dreams.

These examples also sharpened my dreaming. If such success was possible, I came to realize the need to partner with experts who had skills I did not possess. I knew that obtaining business partners with incredible talent was a requirement of my BIG (moon shot) company dreams. I learned that, of course, even Sam Walton had to tap into other resources to get his dreams to skyrocket. After serving in the U.S. Army, Walton took his savings and a loan from his father-in-law to open a Ben Franklin variety store—a five-and-dime arts and craft store chain—in Arkansas.[*] He and his brother eventually owned fifteen franchises, but they had bigger ideas for themselves.

They wanted to open larger stores in rural areas where they believed customers were underserved and needed a loyal brand to rely on. The franchise bosses didn't agree, and they wouldn't back their plan, so the Waltons had to go at it alone. At first, they felt this was a big blow to their big plan, but in hindsight, they saw this was actually a blessing in disguise. Years later, Walton was quoted in *Financial World* magazine explaining that he was happy they rejected him, "because I was forced to build our own team and program." In the wake of his initial rejection, Walton was able to tailor the perfect team to support his massive dream.

In hindsight, Mr. Walton might say, "I couldn't believe my luck" . . . similar to John Pennington and Michael Franzese.

---

[*]   Lee Habeeb, "Sam Walton: The American Underdog/Rebel Who Changed Retail," *Newsweek*, April 5, 2023, https://www.newsweek.com/sam-walton-american-underdog-rebel-who-changed-retail-1792313.

It took years, but with some luck, I ended up with brilliant—and I mean brilliant with a capital "B"—business partners. As a team, we worked synergistically. Our enterprise skyrocketed to one of the premier investment firms in the United States. But, to understand and appreciate how I use probabilities, not predictions, to make business decisions and succeed, it's helpful to understand my beginnings.

I was not a great student in high school. I figured my only way out was sports, with football being my best option. Through my teenage years, I thought I had a real chance of being a professional athlete. I had been captain of the football team, swim team, and baseball team. I had made the school's wrestling team, tennis team, basketball team, and track team (placing first in pole vaulting at a regional meet). One year on the swim team, at every swim meet I entered multiple races —butterfly, freestyle, breaststroke, backstroke, and individual medley races. In that entire year I lost only one single race—by one two-hundredth of a second! By my late teenage years, my strength-to-weight ratio enabled me to bench press double my body weight.

All of this gave me hope for some type of professional athletic future, but then I did a reality check. At five-foot-nine and 175 pounds, my chances of making money as an athlete were one in a million. Not good. Although reality checks can often be depressing, the truth did not discourage me. I wasn't a victim—feeling sorry for myself. This reality check allowed me to accurately assess how deep of a hole I was in and how very far away I was from success. With less-than-optimal grades and no realistic athletic path, I ditched those aspirations and changed paths. Reality was in my face, and I accepted it. Change the path or face defeat.

I remember looking in the mirror and saying: "I am not afraid of being poor, and I am not afraid of being old. I am just afraid of being old and poor at the same time."

Scan the QR code to watch the author discuss the motivational quote that propelled him to success.

Life is not fair, but being born in the United States has counterbalancing advantages. If I could exploit the country's fertile soil for entrepreneurs, I might just have a chance. I needed to find a path, a game, that I could win at. I also had great parents—a father and mother who were great examples of hardworking American stock. They were honest, loving, and supportive parents. What a great thing to have, and I realized it.

But to win, I needed to become an expert in something—say, like the sort of expert LeBron James is at basketball. By most accounts, through his expertise on the basketball court, he's worth somewhere between $500 million and $1 billion. He's an expert at his game. But I knew that had I started playing basketball when I was two years old and played every day for ten hours a day, I would still never have the skill set that he has. I needed to choose another game.

In contrast, the top ten hedge fund managers on Wall Street— the best at their game—earn more than half a billion dollars every year. They make in one year what the best basketball player in the world has acquired in his entire career.

In 1999, I watched a news story that demonized hedge fund managers for their enormous incomes, while also paying less in taxes than those with a fraction of that income. I remember thinking—rather than feeling resentful or jealous—*How can I become a hedge fund manager myself? Could I win at that game?*

Once again, the odds were overwhelming. I knew almost nothing about private equity funds, hedge funds, or real estate limited partnerships. But, in this country, I felt if you gave me enough time and good health, and if I got up every day and tried, then maybe I could win. Looking back, my aspirations, arrogance, and confidence seem ridiculous based on where I was. But each year for the next five years, I worked on it, and the skill sets required to launch my own private equity fund continued to grow. I passed the Series 7 exam, sold mortgages for a while, and later passed the Series 65 exam. This self-education included reading private placement memorandums (PPM) and limited partnership agreements (LPA) in my spare time. I was continually increasing the probability of success. It's somewhat difficult to describe, but here's how I launched my first private equity fund in 2004:

Finding Skill Sets That You Don't Have

First off, I needed investors. More than that, I needed a *pipeline* of investors. This would require the very best sales and marketing skills. I was a good salesman but not a *great* salesman. I needed a great salesman to really make this business take off. I had to find someone who was a born salesman. A person who is so excited to attend a large charity event that he could not sleep the night before. A person who loves chatting up others on the phone. A person who arrives at a charity event half an hour early and is the last one to leave. A natural networker who studies and works hard to master the skill of raising capital. A perfect money raiser. This is just one part of the team that was needed to build a supersized company.

I knew that wasn't me. My attitude was, if I have to attend an event, I'll arrive late, munch on a few fancy snack bites, and leave within forty-five minutes. Was there a person who loved doing that? Did they exist?

I met this person in 2004. I found someone who loved to talk on the phone. Who could not sleep the night before attending a huge charity event or gala. Who could identify the ultrawealthy in a crowd within thirty minutes. Who would have their business cards by the end of the evening, and they would have his.

We didn't stop there. Giving it some thought, we pinpointed three basic skill sets needed to run a successful investment fund:

1. Capital raising
2. Experienced investment officers
3. Back-office operators for accounting, regulations, investor relations, and debt financing

I was good at all three, but we needed *experts*. Not good but *great*. We needed a team with the kind of talent concentration that offered the potential for exponential growth. Building teams (or partnerships) of people with exquisite skill sets who are focused on a common goal is the secret ingredient to most successful companies. They may argue in conference rooms about the direction of the company for hours and hours, but when they leave that room with a defined plan, they're a united front with a unified focus.

A Game We Could Win At

Even though I had yet to realize my dream of starting a private equity fund, I knew I had found a game I could win. In 2004, we began to offer real estate short-term lending, cobbling together five or six investors to capitalize a real estate loan (a syndicated deal). Each and every deal was a lot of work, going out and talking to new investors for each transaction.

I began to appreciate how complex it was to develop and launch a fund. It reminded me of something I once heard a NASA scientist say: "Complexity is the enemy of reliability. They can work together, but they constantly fight one another." There was no book, no online course, and no experienced x-fund manager that would teach me exactly how to start my own fund. Still, over those five years (1999 to 2004), I gradually acquired both the knowledge and the confidence to put that understanding toward creating that fund.

Then it happened. One transaction changed our future. One particular deal was set to close on a Friday by 5:00 p.m. One key investor didn't wire their funds on time to the title company. We lost the deal. Months of work, time, and energy for naught. Extremely frustrated, mad, and embarrassed, we needed a break. Looking back on this event, "I couldn't believe my luck." We flew down to Ecuador for scuba diving. On the return trip, the flights were mangled, and we had a fourteen-hour layover in Miami. To make the most of the day, we went to a nice resort, sat by the pool, and talked about the future. We ran probabilities, and I once again laid out my five years of planning to start a private equity fund.

Then my business partner asked me: "When are we going to start our own fund?" I spent the next four hours going over all the things we would need to do to start, run, and succeed as fund managers. It was a long list:

- Producing quarterly reports
- Deciding on an American or European waterfall system (the method by which capital is distributed to a fund's various investors)
- Choosing the ever-important preferred rate of return
- Developing and building out a strict protocol for the investment committees
- Filing the fund with the SEC
- Hiring a third-party CPA firm to perform annual audits
- Developing a compliance structure that would pass any investigation from the SEC, including the IRS or state securities regulators
- Obtaining debt financing

As I said, the list was very long. But once I finished, my partner exclaimed: "John, let's do it!"

Over the next several years, we learned each other's jobs. When he went to pitch investors, I was there. When I went on a two-day trip to underwrite a property, he joined me. When the written quarterly reports were due to our investors, both of us checked and rechecked the calculations and proofread them. We knew we needed redundancy, and the only way to get it was to mirror each other's responsibilities. Long hours and long weeks with only a hope of growth and success. In retrospect, the probability of success was actually quite high because everything for the past five years had been leading up to the culmination of a fund launch.

Over the next several years, additional partners joined the firm, and the talent pool grew exponentially. With such a concentration of skill and ability in one firm, investors began to flood into our group of funds. Honest, hardworking business acumen always attracts investment dollars.

It didn't take very long to learn that we needed three different types of capital raisers: one person to raise capital from high-net-worth individuals, another focusing on family office investors, and a third person covering institutional investors. The supersized business model required three different types of capital-raising skills if we were going to become a unicorn (a billion-dollar business).

Secret to Success:
Brilliant Business Partners and Teamwork

The supersized idea grew to thousands of employees. Despite that large number, we tried to maintain as much consistency as possible when adding new personnel. Whenever I was about to hire a new employee or do any type of company training, I would offer two examples on the subject of team. These were inspired by my business partners who joined the third fund in early 2009 when we were still developing the business model. These brilliant partners were big proponents of the guidance in Jim Collins's classic bestseller *Good to Great*. I latched on to the concepts, as they inspired me. Eventually, I incorporated their team principles and wisdom into the following presentation. When I sensed that an employee was losing the vision of what we were building, I would hit them with these two scenarios.

Team Scenario #1 (Rowboat)

Everyone says they're a team player. Are they, or are they just saying that? Like judging the Fed, I observe actions versus words. Imagine that we are in the middle of the

Pacific Ocean in a twenty-person rowboat. We do not know exactly where we are. We have limited supplies of water and food. I stand up and announce that I have studied the stars and the ocean currents, and I believe we are about 400 miles from Asia. We should start rowing west. You stand up and declare that you have also studied the ocean currents and the stars. You believe we are only 200 miles from California, and we should start rowing east.

We debate vigorously, but we cannot debate for long. Again, we have limited supplies. A vote is taken. Four people vote to row toward Asia, and sixteen people vote to row toward California. The team has made a decision. In my heart, I believe we are thousands of miles from California. Since I am a team player, what do I do? To be a true team player, there can be no murmuring, no negative talk, or fomenting doubt about the team's decision. I can't drag my paddle in the water, protesting to slow the boat down. I have two choices: (i) row diligently toward California, even though I believe it is the wrong direction; or (ii) jump off the boat and start swimming toward Asia. That is what it means to be a team player.

Team Scenario #2 (Football Super Bowl)

We are on a professional football team playing in the Super Bowl. There is one second on the clock, the ball is on the one-yard line, and we are losing by four points. The only way to win is to score a touchdown.

Your position is left tackle. Today, that means your job is to block the best defensive lineman in the league. You have been doing a fantastic job all game. I am the quarterback.

We are in the huddle, and the play comes in from the coach on the sideline. The play is running back sweep left.

One big problem: We have run this play several times today, and it hasn't worked. In the huddle, you argue that the play is just going to fail again. You ask me to change the play. But the team decides to call running back sweep left, the huddle breaks, and we go to the line. You're still upset. You just do not believe in the play. But you know the game film is going to catch everything you do—if you don't give the play your best shot, everyone will know it. Moreover, you know if this play does not work, there will be no Super Bowl championship ring on your finger.

It comes down to two choices: You need to either take yourself out of the game and call in a substitute, or you need to block like you have never blocked before. (Confession: Any time I have difficulty explaining something, I always give a football analogy, because everyone understands football—or thinks they do.)

After giving these two scenarios, I always remind everyone—we are not playing tennis, and we are not playing golf. This company is a team sport. You are encouraged to argue all you want in a conference room. In fact, you need to argue your point with other people in the firm. It builds a stronger company and shows that you care enough to make an argument. Sometimes it needs to be a heated debate. But when the decision is made and we all leave that conference room, we must all leave as a united front with a unified plan. There is no going back to your office and bad-mouthing the decision to other employees. There is no murmuring by the water cooler. Either you are a team player, a *true* team player, or you need to take yourself out of the game or get off the boat and swim.

I usually follow this up with an actual scenario. The company has decided to become a reporting company and requires employees to disclose their personal stock trading activities. These personal reports need to be filed online on time every quarter. This is what the company has decided. No one likes doing this. True team players, even though they disagree with this decision, will still row robustly with everyone else. Because it is what the team has decided to do. Will you do this?

Following this training exercise, company personnel were very rarely late completing tasks that they deemed unimportant or even worthless. They knew: Don't claim to be a team player unless you really are one. The company made this team temperament resonate from the board of directors to the newest employee hired. One of my business partners eventually translated this into a culture of, "We just get it done, done, done"—no matter what "it" is.

Dissent and Diversifying

A business partner of mine used to have the following quote on his desk:

> *"If you and I agree all of the time on every issue, then one of us is unnecessary."*
> —William Wrigley, Jr.

How true! Disagreement is fundamental to building a large business. Books are written to support the value of new and different perspectives. And, by definition, you and I are never going to agree perfectly on every single point. Nor should we.

Disagreement and debate are not enemies of team players. In fact, anything but. The fact that someone devotes thought and energy to offering a different perspective or idea shows they are truly vested in the success of the group as a whole. It's important to stress that in the context of a discussion of what it means to be a team player. Debate and contesting opinions with a unified resolve is one ingredient needed for the makings of a great company. In other words, you need them to form and sustain a great team.

In fact, the book that you're reading now is very much open to debate, if you happen to have differing viewpoints. Bear in mind this material is an eclectic computation of various questions and my answers. They are not "the" answer but rather "an" answer. Varied viewpoints serve to strengthen discourse and, in turn, produce more complete and better-thought-out solutions.

Diversifying can take other forms for those looking to achieve success. When I serve as a mentor to someone, I always raise the point that they need at least three mentors. Absorb three different opinions from three people you believe can help you, internalize those three perspectives, grind on the ideas, organize the thoughts, and then formulate your own unique implementation.

By contrast, never assume that you can do it exactly like your mentor did it. That is flawed thinking. Because your situation and timing are NEVER the same. Your challenges or hurdles are never exactly like someone else's. Therefore, do not assume that anyone—and I mean anyone—has the exact answer you are looking for. You have to accommodate all perspectives and then make your own business decision. Then use probabilities to decide on a path.

That's why a team comprised of genuine team players is such a valuable component of boxing in success. Team players don't accept a team plan until it's decided on—until then, they know the value of dissent and discussion. It enables success by effectively preventing the business from being boxed in—boxed in by agreement by conditioning, an unwillingness to question, or, yes, fear of going against a crowd. And once that team arrives at a decision, the odds of controlling outcomes increase. No predictions . . . just probabilities.

Keep at It, No Matter What

Transferring knowledge to a younger generation is gratifying for older people. It makes us Boomers feel like we had a life of value when someone else can shorten their learning curves from our missteps and successes. People want to hear about the business winners, but a great deal of business acumen is learned from failure. All my missteps have taught me something more about business—what it takes, when to take risks, and when to be conservative.

And here's something I have told my kids since they were teenagers: There are people who move to the United States from Nigeria or Thailand who don't speak a word of English; they are forced to make a life for themselves in an utterly foreign environment. Yet, within three years, they owned two restaurants and a few laundromats.

How can they do this? For one thing, it's because the United States is like a farmer in a field of nutrient-rich, perfectly plowed soil. The United States has all the ingredients for business success. As I said before, the day you are born in the U.S.A. or the day you move to the U.S.A. is the day you won the lottery for entrepreneurs.

Here's the simple bit of wisdom I drilled into my kids' heads—a simple formula:

1. Stay healthy.
2. Wake up every day and try—not just five days a week but seven.
3. You will eventually succeed in the United States of America.

It's academic: 1 + 2 = 3.

In my case, I was able to stay healthy and got up every day and tried and tried again, eventually succeeding. My goal was not to make every single business idea work. My overarching goal was to be a self-made successful businessperson. There were nights I went to bed crying on my big pillow because things just were not working out. But it did not matter—as long as I got up the next morning and tried, I could eventually succeed.

I have friends who are not healthy and are very successful. You can be successful and unhealthy at the same time. I am not saying you cannot do this. But my formula is academic—one plus two equals three. This protects and promotes your personal number one product. That product being *you*. It places you in greater control. Good health strengthens both protection and control.

One last bit of wisdom to pass along. Owning and running a business is about getting things done—not 98 percent done but 100 percent. Done with a capital "D." Occasionally, the last 2 percent takes as long to complete as the first 98. This is why construction contractors rarely take over and finish someone else's job. Because the project looks 98 percent complete, it seems as though it should be done in a few weeks. That can turn into several months. The most successful business owners really know how to complete tasks fully—100 percent each and every time.

They know the essential value of sticking with something, getting up every day and trying—over and over, if need be. They keep at it, no matter what. If you do the same, you'll find the success you seek, too.

Here are some organizations that all have a common, fundamental, unified goal—the best of the best: the Fed, the SEC, the IRS, the U.S. military, Congress, and the U.S. president. When brought together, this assembled team enables things that seem to be impossible to become reality.

If we want to have a successful family, marriage, or company, treat it as a team. Align its interests as a team and promote continued reinvention and excellence as a team. It's amazing what can happen when given the opportunity to learn from the best, the GOATs. That way, we can all learn how a team created the greatest product of all time—and apply that wisdom to our own lives.

BOXING IN BASICS

8A. Boxing in competitors requires a closely aligned team that works together in a consistently focused, unified manner.

8B. Seek out team members with strong, complementary skills. Look for people who excel at things you may not do nearly as well.

8C. All teams have disagreements. In fact, disagreement is healthy, as it leads to better-thought-out decisions. But once that decision is made, everyone involved must act as a team player. The time for dissension has passed.

8D. Always work toward completing every job 100 percent. Jobs that go unfinished tend to stay unfinished or worse, completed with a less than ideal outcome.

8E. The organizations that have boxed in Bitcoin represent the ideal prototype of teamwork and execution. Embrace their form of teamwork in your life, both personal and professional.

PART THREE

Building the Wealth Machine

CHAPTER 9
With Real Intent

I made one single change in my life that became the key to becoming a successful entrepreneur. I still use it today with almost every challenge that is placed before me. At first glance, it will appear trivial. But I assure you, this *one thing* was the key that unlocked the doors to my success.

Deep down inside, becoming successful was embedded within my overreaching desire. I really intended to succeed but lacked the right formula. Finding a fundamental approach that would increase the probability of coming out on top became a worry that grated on my mind continually. Then I asked myself: *What does "real intent" really mean?*

There are more than seven billion people on the planet. That means there are more than seven billion ways to solve problems. Not wrong ways, just *different* ways. Business is about solving problems. With that in mind, allow me to offer one way to solve problems, one perspective that has worked for me time and time again.

First, assume that the human mind is constantly working. It never really shuts all the way off. It's akin to a computer that continually consumes a steady stream of power. It's always there, waiting for someone to ask it a question. For those who understand computers, the way a question is phrased can produce totally different results and outputs. If you ask your mind a question that is negative in nature, you're probably going to get an answer that isn't so optimistic. But a negatively phrased question rarely offers an actual solution. Negative questions inevitably prompt worthless answers. The answer can do you no good and is of no value to the person—you—who asked it.

An example would be something like this: *Why am I so stupid?* Have you ever asked that? I have! I've done it myself many times—you most likely have as well. Interestingly enough, that question—however absurd—does lead to another question: *Why would anyone ask that, possibly over and over again, when the answer is inevitably of no use at all?*

This is why it is important to phrase questions that are meant to solve problems in a way that opens our brains up to do what they do best: find solutions.

Let's look at another example, the question: *Why can't I learn the new computer program at work?* Think about all the possible answers to that question. There may be many of them, but each and every one would be negative in nature. All they would do is reinforce all the reasons why I *can't* learn that program. It would also solidify my belief that I will never be able to learn it—all because my mind answered the actual question I asked it.

Let's apply this discussion to Boxing In Bitcoin. Do you think that the U.S. government essentially asked itself: *Why are we so stupid that we can't box in this threat to our number one product?* Of course not. Instead, they likely asked: *How can we learn how to box in Bitcoin?* And the answer was simple—*Let's talk to JPMorgan and learn exactly how they controlled the precious metals markets for all those years.*

The solution is just as straightforward for every entrepreneur. Each of us needs to learn to phrase our questions positively to produce answers that benefit us. For instance, instead of asking why we can't learn the computer program, we should ask, *How can I learn the new computer program at work?* That way, when the brain answers the question, *How I can learn it?*, then an action list comes to life. Action lists always improve the probability of success.

The answer might be:

- You **can** learn the new program by asking one of your coworkers to help you.
- You **can** learn the new program by purchasing an online tutorial.
- You **can** learn the new program by taking a computer class at a college.
- You **can** learn the new program by reading a book on computers.

All of these answers enable the ability to overcome the problem. That's what I mean by asking questions with real intent. The answers also reinforce the belief that computer programs can be learned. Asking negative questions gives answers that disable the positive and reinforce the negative. On the other hand, positive questions addressing how someone can overcome an obstacle will arm that person with a to-do list.

A to-do list is an empowering action list, especially when the list builds toward reaching a big goal. As a result, it accelerates your progress in becoming something that you currently are not. The miracle in all this is not in helping humans to see themselves as they are but rather in helping them envision themselves as what they *can become.*

I already know what I am. I already know that I am an idiot—sometimes, at least. But what I really want to know is, how can I become smart? That is what I want to understand and learn—this is my true core goal. How can I become something that I am not? This was the change I made in my life. It was my key to success. The fun thing about this is each person can reprogram their mind to learn how to become something more than they currently are. Isn't that concept truly elevating?

There's another point relating to Boxing In Bitcoin that pertains here. Although many would look at the government's actions as self-serving and mercenary, it's important to remember all the good the preeminence of the dollar has done. Jobs. Prosperity. Worldwide poverty reduction. Greater security around the world.

The same dynamic applies here. Most humans are selfish, and they know it. Staying that way is not destiny. Applying real intent to escaping that state of mind is exalting. The mind is programmable. Becoming a better person—who cares for and loves their fellow humans and all other life forms—might all come down to how you phrase questions.

For instance, replacing *Why can't I become wealthy?* with *How can I become wealthy?* might seem greedy and self-centered. But that question, if used to help others, becomes a question that ultimately blossoms into generosity and charity. As I said, it all depends on how questions are phrased that reveals the real intent.

An "Expert" on Private Equity Funds

My sons used to tease me a bit, posing pointed questions such as "Dad, you are not really an expert on real estate. How is it that you are a co-founder and fund manager of a multi-billion-dollar family of real estate funds?"

Their assessment is correct. I'm not a real estate expert. However, I am an expert on private equity funds. Here's how I answered their teasing-but-relevant question, using a baseball metaphor.

I am a good capital raiser. I am not a fantastic capital raiser. I am a good baseball pitcher but far short of the star power needed to win consistently. Still, I have a lifetime goal of earning a World Series championship ring. The question is: ***How can I*** *earn a World Series championship ring?*

A team that wins a World Series needs a pitcher who can throw a 98-mile-an-hour fastball. Rather than ask *How can I get on a team like that?*, I decided to start my own team and then attract World Series–caliber talent. I did this by asking: *How can I attract this type of talent? What would appeal to a player with a 98-mile-an-hour fastball to join my baseball team? What can I do?*

Most baseball players do not know how to build a state-of-the-art baseball stadium with the best audio-visual features, the best hotdogs, great seating, and parking. Most baseball players do not know how to land the best television contracts for massive viewership and revenue during the season—money that helps pay their exorbitant salaries. Most baseball players do not understand what the purpose of a negotiator really is.

I really intend to earn a World Series championship ring. What **can I** do? What is possible, if not probable? If I build the best baseball stadium with the best media contracts, could I attract the best players? Will a pitcher with a 98-mile-an-hour fastball play on my team for a little less compensation if he's going to receive fantastic multimedia coverage that he can leverage in the future? If I build a Major League Baseball stadium and franchise, could I give up some of the ownership in that venture to attract and sign incredible talent? Could I have a profit-sharing program for the players? The better hot dog sales are, the more money we all make by aligning our interests. When the gift shop sells baseball jerseys, the players share in the profits. Would that lure talent? Incredible talent?

I am the owner, pitcher, and manager with a BIG dream. The team is winning some but losing too many to become a champion. I still need to attract that pitcher with a 98-mile-an-hour fastball. My strategy is to offer what others will not—ownership in the franchise. I landed an All-Star pitcher—fantastic! I then moved out to play center field. With a fantastic pitcher, we are winning more games. As a result, we are now able to sign a truly great defensive center fielder with 4.2-second speed in the 40-yard dash and an arm like Roberto Clemente. We started winning even more games.

This scenario repeats as we build a championship team. By now, I have switched to playing second base. I am an average, solid player. But the rest of my team are genuine studs. They all make the All-Star team. They have come together, thanks to something many other teams do not have—an alignment of interests! Each player is motivated, working in the same direction for the same goals. That's because each player has a vested interest in the success of the team, on the field and in its financial success. They are all equity owners of a professional baseball team.

I did not make the roster of the best team in the world because I was the best second baseman. I am on the roster because I could do things other people could not do or did not want to do—build stadiums, land television contracts, negotiate, get the best hot dogs for the fans, and structure things so that the best players in the world, if they joined the team, benefitted financially, no matter if it was from television revenue or sales of jerseys. The real talent are the baseball players. The real talent of our private equity funds are the brilliant business partners. Everyone has a special position to play in order to work as a team and create greatness.

Staying healthy and pulling in the same direction, these players start to function as a true "team." Naturally, they disagree about many things. They argue in the clubhouse about the direction the organization should go. But when the team makes a decision and exits the clubhouse, they push forward as a united front for excellence on and off the field. They work as a team. Again, this is not golf or tennis—it is a *team* sport.

This scenario is similar to starting and running a highly successful private equity investment fund. I was a good capital raiser, but I needed a *fantastic* capital raiser. I could underwrite and assess the fair value of a twenty-unit apartment complex, but I needed fantastic talent (a chief investment officer) who could underwrite and assess the fair value of a 1,200-unit apartment community. How can talent like that be acquired? How can a company attract the best talent? If you are not the most seasoned real estate investor, then find talent that can build a company that is a magnet for even greater talent.

Teams of highly successful talent can accomplish astonishing feats. The best stockbrokers (ones with an Ivy League degree and a job on Wall Street) think about the same thing each day when they drive to work: *One day I am going to start my own investment fund.* The top real estate commercial mortgage underwriter who works for a national bank thinks the same thing during their daily commute: *In a few years, I want to start my own real estate investment fund.*

What stands between the player with a 98-mile-an-hour fastball and a World Series championship ring? They need a great team, in the front office as well as the back, with an aligned interest. They need a business structure that embodies excellence in every way. The point is, there is not just one path to earning a World Series championship ring. Nor, in response to my sons' question, is there just one path to being a part of an extremely large real estate family of private equity investment funds, managing tens of billions U.S. dollars from investors all over the world.

These are all examples of "with real intent." Expecting to win, then the intention of your questions—*How can I?*—reveals the real intention of success. It shows that you truly intend to triumph. Before we go on, I really need to emphasize how essential the ideas of "finding things that fit" or "seeking to find things that fit" are to business success.

In like manner, people in business whom you respect will often tell you that you can't do something. They stress "can't" because it's possible they don't know everything you know. They may be older and wiser than you, but they have not specifically experienced everything you have.

Similarly, you are not a good enough baseball player to make the cut on a World Series baseball team. Your resume is not good enough to warrant employment at a top private equity hedge fund. When I co-founded each of my fourteen businesses, there was always someone telling me why it would not succeed. From their perspective they viewed me as I was, but I had a vision of not what I was but rather what I *could become*. This was particularly true with my most successful venture. This is a fact of life that everyone needs to program their mind to deal with by asking *How **can** we succeed?* in the face of others' skepticism. Bitcoin wasn't boxed in by a single organization. It required a team effort focused on protecting and promoting their number one product.

Your likelihood of success will improve exponentially if you have a great group of "team-minded" individuals. Don't try to predict the future. Instead, improve the path of successful probabilities. Seek to build a great team that attracts even better team members and box in the probability of success. And, once it's boxed in, don't allow success to escape. No predictions, just probabilities.

BOXING IN BASICS

9A. When considering any problem or situation, asking the right type of question can mean the difference between an answer that makes things possible or one that merely reinforces negativity. This is what I refer to when I talk about questions "with real intent."

9B. Don't ask yourself why you're so slow or so stupid. Instead, ask how you can become more mentally agile and more insightful. That produces a to-do list that builds toward success.

9C. A variant of this is attaching a negative connotation to something that doesn't have to be bad. Asking how you can become rich may seem self-serving, but many rich people have been able to help society in many ways.

9D. Look to build an organization where excellence is the rule, rather than the exception. That involves attracting the best talent and creating loyalty to and support for the group's success.

CHAPTER 10

Raising Capital for Domination—Size Matters

Traveling to the United States Capitol to raise some United States capital? Then you'll need to know the difference between *capitol* and *capital*. Nothing will get you kicked out of a prospective investor's office faster than putting *capitol* instead of *capital* on one of your PowerPoint pitchbook slides. Credibility? Extinguished in a nanosecond.

Joking aside, raising investment dollars from potential investors is a difficult thing to do. Think of 200 people from high school. Of those 200, how many do you think could be a very successful capital raiser for an investment fund? The answer is very few. Convincing someone to scratch a check in the hundreds of thousands—maybe more? The people who can accomplish that are few and far between. It is a rare skill set.

The U.S. government had a windfall of gold flowing into this country during World War I and World War II because they were selling everything under the sun to the warring countries. The United States had obtained more than 60 percent of the world's gold reserves by 1944. Golden Rule number one is *do unto others as you want them to do unto you*. Golden Rule number two is *he who has all the gold makes all the rules*. Therefore, it's essential to learn to raise vast sums of capital, enabling yourself to be the rule-maker instead of a rule-taker.

As my sons grew into teenagers, I told them that they had to follow two paths if they wanted to make a lot of money:

- Do something that no one wants to do.
- Do things others cannot do.

As to the first path, there's a lot of money to be made in garbage collection, but few want that profession. No one wants to attend a twenty-year high school class reunion and brag about how many tons of trash they collected last month. However, it is a lucrative industry.

Waste Management, Inc.—one of the most well-known disposal services in North America—began in Chicago when Dutch immigrant Harm Huizenga offered to collect and remove waste from Chicago streets for a small fee in 1893. At the time, waste management wasn't a defined process carried out by cities, and trash often piled up on the sides of streets with no collections planned. His operation grew over several decades, but it wasn't until the 1960s when his grandson was running the operation that they saw a major opportunity. The way Americans were consuming products—and throwing away their packaging—was changing. His grandson, Wayne Huizenga, enlisted the help of two investors to catapult his vision into reality. They came up with a scalable plan to help handle the uptick in waste around American cities, and it worked. By the 1980s, Waste Management had become the world's largest waste disposal company.

There are plenty of other profitable paths—from landscaping to plumbing—but there's not a lot of cachet attached to them. That's why many people avoid them. These are professions that most people don't want to do but make a lot of money for those who do choose them. (FYI, as a side note, I am currently a small minority owner of a large waste landfill, and I worked as a plumber's apprentice to get myself through college.)

An example of the second path is an orthodontist who can do things that dentists can't do; therefore, the orthodontist makes more money on average. A heart surgeon can do things that a general practitioner can't, so more dollars find their way to the heart surgeon.

The same thing is true with sales and raising capital. As I taught my sons years ago, some of the highest-paid people in the world are salesmen. The reason is that they do things other people cannot do. And raising capital from potential investors requires a skill set that very few people command. By definition, they get paid a lot of money for their singular abilities.

A successful long-term career raising capital requires one key ingredient above all else: a sound and long-lasting successful investment product. Without a good investment track record, even the best capital raiser in the world will, in effect, start spelling *capitol* instead of *capital* and be shown the door. As I've said before, people pay attention to what you've done, not what you say.

Most salesmen feel like hired guns. They pop into a company for a while to increase revenue. They don't receive any ownership, they get paid very well, then they move on to the next company. Bopping around from company to company, product to product, they nail huge commissions for a short period of time, then go elsewhere. This is often the life that capital raisers find themselves in.

Salespeople with great skill sets rarely find a permanent home with long-term horizons. I knew if I ever found a fantastic capital raiser, I would want to make them a partner with long-term equity. I would make certain to help manufacture fantastic products and investments that they could be proud of and sell to investors with confidence. I would love to turn the entire dynamic on its ear, offering a long-term successful career at one investment shop as opposed to someone who pops up to boost sales or capital raising whenever the company needs a new marketing strategy. I wanted them to stay and become a part of something valuable. Here are a few strategies to accomplish this outcome.

The Clawback

There are few strategies better than the "clawback" to keeping great capital raisers in a company. Many investment funds will try to attract successful capital raisers with a step-up compensation plan. For example, if you raise $1 million, you will receive 1 percent of general partnership ownership; raise $5 million, 5 percent; $10 million, 10 percent.

The clawback is different. It's much more effective. Here's how it works: We believe you're such a great capital raiser that we are going to give you 15 percent ownership in the general partnership today, this very minute. The provision is that you raise us $20 million in the next twelve months. If you do, you retain your 15 percent ownership. If you only raise $10 million, then we will claw you back to 8 percent ownership; much the same if you only raise $5 million, you receive 3 percent.

Think about what this person is going to tell their spouse that night: "Honey, I have just been made a 15 percent owner in a private equity fund!" Of course, they never bring up the clawback provision because they know they are going to raise the $20 million—the clawback is irrelevant in a great salesperson's mind. Their demeanor changes. They walk and talk and act as they should . . . as an equity owner of a firm. Moreover, extending this type of compensation plan is pure motivation—they'll work like they never have before to retain (not receive) that sweet 15 percent cut of "equity." The American dream = "equity."

The beautiful thing about general partnership and limited partnership structures is that a closed-end fund is not forever. Since only a limited number of shares (units) are sold, there is a time limit on the life of the fund. If this capital raiser doesn't work out, then you probably won't want them involved in any subsequent funds. But if they are successful in raising capital for the first fund, you'll really want them around for the launch of funds number two and three. In effect, production creates additional equity ownership. That's a novel proposal for a salesperson, but it's extremely intriguing—and attractive.

This clawback strategy stabilizes the capital raising arm of the company—a never-ending and long-lasting business model for growth. That's something very few firms ever obtain. The clawback effectively changes the mindset of everyone on the team. From day one, they have specific and quantitative goals and objectives that must be met to maintain their equity ownership. It aligns interests and taps into the entrepreneurial spirit within them—a piece of equity in the company. Enabling them to obtain the American dream.

Too Young to Raise Capital?

"I'm too young to raise capital." That's what my twenty-two-year-old son said as I was trying to convince him that starting and managing a limited partnership was one of the best opportunities in the United States. But, as we all know, that requires the raising of capital from investors to accomplish the objectives of the investment thesis. And my son insisted no investor was going to give a twenty-two-year-old college student any money.

So, I presented to him a hypothetical:

- I know a lady in Montana who needs to sell her Lamborghini by Saturday for $100,000 cash. I've already had my top mechanic check the car out, and it's perfect.
- I have a buyer in California who is willing to pay $250,000. He's staked a $10,000 deposit. He wants the car delivered in the next two weeks.
- The woman in Montana must have the $100,000 by noon on Saturday.
- Can you, my twenty-two-year-old son, find the $100,000 cash for a guaranteed profit of $150,000 in the next two weeks?

My son thought about it for a minute: "Yeah," he answered slowly, "I think I could put it together—$100,000 by this Saturday."

I asked him where he would go, who he would talk to, and what would be his pitch. He listed his business professors at college, old football coaches, and his rich uncle and aunt. He said he would talk to everybody because it's a sure deal.

"There it is," I announced with satisfaction.

"What are you talking about?" he asked.

"Well, five minutes ago you told me that no one would give a twenty-two-year-old kid in college a lot of money for investment. Now you're saying you could definitely raise $100,000 by this Saturday. What has changed in the last five minutes?"

I didn't give him a chance to answer.

"The deal is so good that anyone would invest in something like that," I said. "There it is. You have a great deal, and with a great deal, you believe you can raise the money, correct?"

He agreed.

"So, it's not that you cannot raise money," I went on. "It is just that you haven't found a great deal to warrant your effort—to enable you to believe in your product."

He quickly nodded in agreement.

"The dilemma is that you need a lucrative deal," I said. "All you need to do is go and find a great deal with a lucrative outcome—that solves the dilemma of raising capital. Stop finding marginal deals and go out and find a fantastically solid deal. That way, you can make money by starting your own investment fund."

To his credit, he did just that. He went out and started his own private equity limited partnership. He raised capital, deployed capital, and made great returns for his investors—all while he was in college. He was able to change his past and become something that he was not before by simply asking *How can I start a fund?* instead of *Why can't I figure out how to start a fund?*

He transitioned from a fixed mindset to a growth mindset. And what he discovered was the essence of life itself—that is, not just knowing who you are but what you can become. Previously, he was not a capital raiser. But knowing what you are is never as good as knowing *what you can become.* By developing skill sets that other people rarely obtain, he stopped asking who he was and started asking what he could become.

In the English language, the words "history" and "story" have two separate meanings. However, within the German language, they have one single word for both meanings. Because German children are taught that all history is told from a perspective. They're taught that ten people can see the exact same event in history, then explain that event from ten different perspectives—and each and every one can be 100 percent correct. Therefore, the Germans have no need for two words here. The word "history" and the word "story" exude the same meaning. All history is a story (or, if you break down the word, all history is "his-story" (or "her-story") from the individual's perspective or point of view. This is why the formation of the word is spelled the way it is—his-story.

Anyone can change their story. Here's a great example of someone transitioning their self-beliefs to empower themselves for a better life.

- **Q:** Who are you?
- **A:** I'm a high-school dropout. I just quit school.
- **Q** (**one year later**): Who are you?
- **A:** I work for a charity downtown, and we raise money for kids who are underprivileged. I'm also a high-school dropout.
- **Q** (**three Years later**): Who are you?
- **A:** I'm the top car salesman at one of the largest dealerships in the state, and I raise money for a charity that helps underprivileged kids. I am also a high-school dropout.
- **Q** (**ten years later**): Who are you?
- **A:** I'm an entrepreneur who started my own private equity fund that imports exotic cars with forty-five employees. As a hobby, I raise capital for a fantastic charity that provides meals and housing for underprivileged children. That's who I am.

This person changed their story by asking what they could become. What are the possibilities? By waking up every day and trying to be the best person that they could be, they eventually changed their story to where dropping out of high school was no longer an integral part of who they were; it wasn't a part of their identity any longer because they had built up so many other positive aspects around it. That's who they used to be a long time ago—history.

No Management Fee

My first two investment funds did not charge an annual management fee to investors. No one had ever heard of us, and our strategy was to get their attention. To do so, we had no management fees. We only wanted to be paid if the investment performed. We only wanted to make money by sharing in the profit, thus referred to as a "performance fee." This meant we only made money after our investors made a preferred rate of return.

The Fed (in its earlier iteration) implemented the same strategy around the world. The Fed will make massive amounts of money but only after the U.S. dollar is accepted everywhere and enables U.S. citizens to obtain wealth. When the Fed began in the early twentieth century, its task was figuring out how to get other countries to accept their freshly printed currency. They needed adoption worldwide. Once that was achieved, the Fed's owners would be wealthy. If they failed in worldwide adoption, then they may be mildly wealthy, but eventually the country would not survive without a way to transact commerce internationally. Anytime there is a new product introduced on the planet, for it to be a super success, it needs insatiable demand. And that takes extremely smart people to implement. Learning from the best, and knowing we were new to the investment world, our supersized business needed a similar strategy.

Using investor funds pooled together with our own, we would make asset-backed loans on real estate, charging origination points to the borrowers with an appropriate interest rate. The revenue from the loan could not and would not be distributed to the general partners (my partners and I) until after the loan was paid off and the investors made a minimum 8 percent annual percentage yield—the preferred rate. We, as general partners, only received compensation on profits earned above the preferred rate. Once the 8 percent level was met, we earned our performance fee through a very profitable waterfall arrangement. For example, a 20 percent return would be divided; 16 percent for investors; my partners and I received the remaining 4 percent.

It was an exceptional system at the time, attracting many investors to our real estate lending funds—Bridge Loan Capital Fund, LP (2004) and Bridge Loan Capital Fund II, LP (2007). We nicknamed them BLoC I and BLoC II. This strategy gave us a competitive advantage. The question was how we could get in front of large-check writers who were accredited investors (someone who is allowed to invest in private securities offerings that are exempt from registration with the SEC). How could we find these people, and then how could we get an appointment and pitch all the great reasons why they should invest with us?

High-net-worth individuals will usually have multiple employees—gatekeepers—who are there to discourage salespeople such as us. You know the script. The phone rings, an assistant answers, you ask to speak to the accredited investor, and the employee says he or she is tied up and asks if they can take a message. This is a common dilemma for most would-be capital raisers. How did we get over this wall? Here's how:

"My name is John Pennington. Your boss does not know me, but this Friday night I've got box seats at an NBA game where the Lakers are playing the Utah Jazz. This comes with dinner and a huge dessert bar at halftime, offered by a gourmet chef—wearing white gloves, of course! My partner and I would like to invite your boss and their partner to join us. Here's my phone number. I am the general partner at Bridge Loan Capital Fund, LP."

What do you think would happen to that employee if they did not deliver that message to their boss ASAP—in five minutes or less? We took a lot of people to NBA games and spent three to four quality hours with them. We learned about their businesses, they learned about our business, and we eventually landed them as investors. Additionally, through their influence, we were able to springboard to other potential investors. We didn't stop there. In addition to other steps, we attended investor functions to further build our network. These and other activities were critical in raising capital for our first investment funds.

Placement Agent Fees

We were as aggressive as we could be in assembling our business and our network of investors. But there are limits to how aggressive one can be. When building up a business, it's essential to be aware of these pitfalls. One such caveat has to do with placement agents and their fees. A *placement agent* is a hired company that sells securities for compensation. A stock brokerage firm (broker/dealer) fits this definition. They receive a commission for their services, known as a *placement agent fee*. The securities laws at the federal and state levels regulate this industry, which can include stocks, bonds, mutual funds, and ownership positions in limited partnerships and limited liability companies.

In most cases the individual is a stockbroker with a Series 7 license. In recent years, a new Series 82 license has become available for individuals who *only* want to receive commissions on the sale of "limited partnership" interests. Like a Series 7 person, a Series 82 representative must be supervised by a broker/dealer. Series 7 and Series 82 persons are prohibited from selling any securities product unless their broker/dealer has preapproved that individual investment. Needless to say, this is a *highly* regulated industry.

If a friend who owns a large company ever says to you, "Hey, I'm selling pieces of my company. If you find someone who buys stock, I'll pay you a commission," you both are likely violating U.S. securities laws. This happens almost every day somewhere across America. It is a common mistake because most people do not understand that selling a piece of a company is selling a security—and receiving a payment for such is something you need a license to do.

It's no different than if your friend is a real estate agent and you find a purchaser for a home they're listing. Legally, your friend cannot pay you a commission, because you do not have a real estate license. The same is true for the sale of securities. SEC regulations are complex, and placement agent fees are often misunderstood. Protect yourself by knowing ways you can legally work with investors.

Commission vs. Performance Fee

"Commission" involves a salesman getting paid for selling an investment to an investor (placement agent fee). A "performance fee" is earned only after the investment does well; it is a share in the profits on the backend.

Another consideration in raising capital is the sort of legal obligation the person doing the actual selling may have—and how they are paid. Under SEC regulations, a stockbroker with a Series 7 license receives a commission for selling a piece of a company. Once the transaction is done, they receive their commission. That's where their legal responsibilities end. Once the transaction is complete, the stockbroker does not need to—or is not required to—perform any other function.

This commission is sometimes confused with an investment advisor fee. An investment advisor doesn't earn their fee by selling securities. An investment advisor usually has a Series 65 license. That allows them to receive compensation for advising others on what securities to purchase or sell on their own. Series 65 people derive their fee from advising, not from transactions. Additionally, a Series 65 advisor cannot receive a "placement agent fee" or commission for the sale of company stock or interests in a limited partnership. They are investment advisors, not brokers.

Thus, a Series 7 person is not a fiduciary—a Series 65 advisor is. That means a Series 7 broker only has to provide you with a "fair" deal, such as an appropriate price. But a Series 65 advisor must provide you with the "best" deal for you, even if that deal is detrimental to the Series 65 person's compensation. They are bound to act in your best interests. A Series 7 broker is not.

If a general partner of a limited partnership fund signs a contract with a broker/dealer to sell its securities, the fund will pay the commission (placement agent fee) to the broker/dealer directly. Once an investor purchases an interest in the limited partnership, the broker/dealer's job is complete. The limited partnership will send the placement agent fee (commission) to the broker/dealer. In turn, the broker/dealer will then pay their Series 7 (or sometimes Series 82) persons for the successful transaction.

Tax ramifications also play a part in this. It's essential that the limited partnership pay placement fees directly to a broker/dealer. Here's why: Placement agent fees are non-deductible business expenses under Internal Revenue Code Section 709(a) if paid from the management fee. That means if the fund pays the general partner for management fees and the general partner then sends a check to the broker/dealer for selling pieces of the limited partnership, this is classified as a "non-deductible business expense." The general partner cannot write that expense off against yearly profits, increasing tax liability.

Let's say the limited partnership pays the general partner a $1 million annual management fee—this is the general partner's income. Then the general partner pays a $1 million commission (placement agent fee) to the broker/dealer for bringing in investors to the limited partnership. Under IRS rules, the general partner cannot write off the $1 million expense and must pay tax on the $1 million in income.

That's a double whammy. In effect, the general partner received $1 million and then paid out $1 million—the general partner ends up with zero dollars in their bank account. Even worse, when income tax season arrives, the general partner has a "phantom profit" of $1 million—remember, they received $1 million in income and then turned around and paid $1 million in placement agent fees. They are still required to pay tax on that income.

> NOTE TO SELF
> ### Master the Tax Game
> One of the most expensive things in life is taxes. Become a student of them or witness your demise.

The bottom line is to make certain that the limited partnership always pays placement agent fees directly to the broker/dealer. Like I said, securities transactions are complex. It's critical to know how transactions can best be handled to avoid nasty tax consequences.

European Waterfall vs. American Waterfall

I mentioned these two distribution structures earlier when outlining how we were preparing to start our first fund. Let's take a closer look, as these are issues that need to be thought through when raising capital for any large and long-term investment.

With an American waterfall arrangement, the general partners receive their profit (performance fee) as each investment of the portfolio is sold. Under a European waterfall arrangement, the general partners have to wait until the end of the fund's life when all of the assets are sold. Only then can they receive any profits (performance fee). Further, this only occurs if investors in the fund generated its guaranteed preferred rate of return (the pref) for the entire life of the fund.

When raising capital, large institutional investors negotiate with a fund's general partner for a European waterfall to regulate how profits are distributed. Smaller investors will usually accept an American waterfall distribution structure. In a standard eight-year close-ended real estate fund, the general partner usually receives 20 percent of the profits from the investments—again, so long as the fund investments meet a minimum preferred rate of return for the limited partners.

What can happen in a pure American waterfall is that—hypothetically—a fund could own 100 investments. The first fifty investments return a 20 percent internal rate of return (IRR).

However, the remaining fifty investments return a negative 16 percent IRR when sold. If all the investments are equally weighted, the general partner would be the only party to make money. Over the eight-year life of the fund, the investors merely break even.

You can see the drawbacks. The investors are happy with the return on the first fifty investments, but they only break even due to losses with the remaining fifty. Thanks to the American waterfall structure, the general partner keeps the profits from the first fifty investments because those were each sold at a profit of 20 percent.

It's very different from a European waterfall. Here, the general partner can only keep 20 percent of the gains on the entire life of the fund. But, with the European system, the general partner is required to return their profits to the fund from those first fifty profitable investments—a classic clawback, as discussed earlier—considering losses from the latter fifty. Accordingly, since the preferred rate of return has not been met, the investors make a 2 percent profit for the life of the fund and the general partner gets zilch.

The difficulty for a general partner in a European waterfall is that they must work for eight years (life of the fund) before they make even one dollar. This financial situation is usually not enticing enough to warrant many general partners' attention.

One solution is a compromise, by allowing the GP to receive a portion of profits as assets are sold but establish a strict clawback formula if further investments don't go as planned.

Offshore Entities

Anytime in a movie or a book when the firm has offshore entities or bank accounts located in the Bahamas or the Cayman Islands, there is always something dubious going on. It makes for great movie theatrics. But in real life they're not the tax-free dodge portrayed in fiction. Rather, their structure just simplifies the payment of the taxes.

Here's an example: A real estate investment thesis (the "Main Fund") headquartered in the United States is raising capital from non-U.S. citizens. If these investors send their money directly to the Main Fund, then they will be required to file a tax return with the IRS every year for the life of that investment fund.

This is a difficult way to raise capital. Say an investor from France who only reads and writes French (this is important for this example) is being pitched a great U.S.-based real estate investment that is targeted to return a 35 percent IRR per year. Unfortunately, the French citizen realizes that each year for the next eight years—until the properties inside of the fund are sold—he or she will have to file a tax return (in English) to the U.S. Internal Revenue Service. That is a deal killer. Even though the targeted returns are great, the laborious filing of taxes in a different country that speaks an entirely different language is a wall that is just too tall to jump over.

But wait, there is a solution! The general partner has set up an entity in Luxembourg or the Cayman Islands or the Bahamas that aggregates investor capital from non-U.S. citizens into a "feeder fund" and then sends those investment dollars to a Delaware Corporation (the "INC") controlled by the general partner of the fund.

This INC then invests into the Main Fund that purchases United States real estate. The general partner usually controls all three entities: (i) Feeder Fund, (ii) the INC, and (iii) the Main Fund. The feeder fund structure enables the Delaware INC to file one single tax return and then distribute after-tax profits to the offshore feeder fund in Luxembourg, the Cayman Islands, or the Bahamas. Then that entity distributes the profits to all the non-U.S. investors. As a result, one single tax form is filed for the aggregated non-U.S. investors. All taxes are paid, with a lot less paperwork.

The Fed and the IRS make it easy for non-U.S. citizens to deal in their number one product. If you live in Hong Kong and purchase a stock on the New York Stock Exchange and then sell it for a profit, there are no taxes due. But this is not true for a U.S. citizen.

From 1933 to 1971 a non-U.S. person (or country) could trade in U.S. dollars for gold bullion. But this was not true for a U.S. citizen. The Fed and the U.S. Treasury seek to market their number one product worldwide. Selling U.S. Treasuries is another way. In addition, they provide access to the SWIFT wire transfer system. They do everything possible to protect and promote.

Utilizing the U.S. financial structure and tools greatly increases the probability of raising capital internationally. Again, taxes are paid. This scenario does not avoid paying taxes. It just makes it easier to successfully raise capital in foreign lands for real estate equity funds. A U.S. real estate fund that does not purchase property but only provides loans (mortgages) on real estate usually doesn't need this sort of feeder fund structure. The reason is the IRS tax codes for lending are different than for owning real estate. They want investment dollars flowing into America, making their number one product sticky.

With apologies to Hollywood, these jurisdictions (offshore banking) usually require a regimented program to mitigate any money laundering activity when using a feeder fund—including redundancy measures and systems. They also require a designated "Anti Money Laundering Officer" (AMLO) to serve as the point person who is accountable to and files regularly scheduled reports to the offshore authorities. Locations like Luxembourg, the Bahamas, and the Cayman Islands are extremely serious about conforming to their regimen of rules and regulations. This is nothing as insidious or as underhanded as movies make it out to be.

Not surprisingly, offering documents to raise capital becomes exponentially more complicated the wider you cast your net. For our first fund in 2004, the PPM, LPA, and subscription documents cost us a little more than $30,000. It was a simple structure of raising capital exclusively from U.S. investors and providing short-term (one to six months) asset-backed real estate loans for U.S.-only properties. It wasn't too complicated.

When we launched a fund to also raise money from investors all over the world in 2008, those offering documents (PPM, LPA, and Sub Docs) were much more expensive. I am not sure about the exact figure, but my oldest son (my attorney son) has recently worked on international docs costing $100,000 to sometimes well over $2 million. That's because they are much more sophisticated, needing to combine U.S. securities laws with the SEC equivalents in multiple countries and U.S. tax laws with those of other countries. This is no small task. It requires international law firms, which understand all the nuances and translation issues. When choosing to go international, it is optimal to have internal equity-owning business partners who are well-versed attorneys in private equity international tax structures. Aligning interests is one of the keys of success because capital from non-U.S. citizens for real estate ownership is many times more complicated.

Offshore feeder funds require a serious commitment to the world of know-your-customer (KYC) and anti-money laundering (AML) laws. For example, investigating and doing your due diligence on an entity from Brazil that wishes to become an investor in your fund can be daunting. That entity may have individual owners living in the Middle East, Russia, or China. Additionally, verifying if even one of those individuals is on a bad-guy list or from a labeled "terrorist region" is difficult to do. Obtaining clearance through AML regimes and KYC regulations requires the general partner to be particularly knowledgeable and sophisticated.

Referring to an example earlier in this chapter, raising capital to purchase a Lamborghini in Montana and then sell it in California is not too difficult. But raising capital to buy and sell one hundred automobiles a month might require some type of investment fund structure. It all depends on what level your team wants to play at.

However, the beautiful thing about this is that it is all possible and probable in the United States of America. It can happen, it does happen, and it will happen—if you can make a few mental adjustments on strategizing your risk matrix related to your probability tables of success. Once more with feeling: The U.S.A. is the most fertile country in the world for an entrepreneur.

1. Stay healthy.
2. Wake up every day and try.
3. Eventually, you will succeed in the United States of America.

Raising large amounts of capital allows a business to hit economies of scale. This enables negotiating power and thus strengthens the longevity of the enterprise. Just as the Fed has leveraged for years, you can also understand how the power of size can bring you wealth and success. Learn from the greatest product ever, the U.S. dollar. Become a price maker instead of a price taker. This requires the scaling of your enterprise through capital raising. Forget who you are . . . concentrate on what you can become.

BOXING IN BASICS

10A. A basic rule for success is to do things others won't or cannot do.

10B. Once again, don't assume you cannot do something. Rather, think about what you need to learn to be successful.

10C. This applies to various and complicated means of raising capital, paying taxes, doling out profits, and other activities. Make sure your team includes those who know these issues inside and out.

10D. Relying on the connotations of popular culture can be a misleading assumption. For instance, offshore entities are not the sole purview of gangsters and tax evaders. Rather, they merely simplify the ways in which you can attract interested investors and streamline any necessary tax payments. Effective strategies but lousy theater.

10E. Raising large amounts of capital enables negotiating power, increasing success probabilities. One of the easiest ways is to start your own limited partnership fund. Become your own GOAT.

CHAPTER 11

Increasing the Probability of Success

All successful entrepreneurs have a common theme—a focus on the outcome. Method and resources are part of the equation, but the *outcome* is the overriding concentration. And the story of Sears, Roebuck and Co. (commonly known first as Sears and Roebuck, then later as just Sears) exemplifies this statement.

While my sons were growing up, they continually watched me during my entrepreneurial years start several businesses. Their observation helped them develop and nurture their own business acumen and success. One question that they repeatedly peppered me with was, "What is the single most important thing for a successful business to have?"

My answer has always been: Remember Sears and Roebuck.

We have discussed this so many times that when I say "Sears and Roebuck" they know exactly what I mean. The Sears and Roebuck story mirrors most all business success stories. It grasps the difficulties of running a successful partnership as well as understanding the different skill sets needed to accomplish the desired outcome.

Born in 1864, Alvah Curtis Roebuck started his career by designing pocket watches. He was interested in producing the best product on the market. When Mr. Sears met Mr. Roebuck, he saw a man of integrity who would continually seek to produce a quality product; he would focus all his professional power on perfecting his merchandise. That was just his nature. Moreover, this is a necessary skill set for any successful business enterprise—someone had to oversee the product quality.

On the other hand, Richard Warren Sears, born in 1863, had an inherent skill for marketing and sales. Sales-skilled people are always searching for a quality product that can form the basis of a successful business. While seemingly opposite acumens, the combination of the two proved to be an incredible American success story.

Once confident of the supply and quality of the products, Sears could focus on what he did best—what he loved to do, what he was made to do: market, sell, and expand the distribution of products and services all over America. Sears without Roebuck would have stumbled with product problems. Roebuck without Sears would have limped along with mediocre revenue. Together, they became the titans of American retail. They each leveraged the other person's attributes—the perfect partnership. Roebuck ran operations and fulfillment, while Sears oversaw sales and marketing. In business, these are two very important skills to have. Very important. They increase any enterprise's success probability.

Was Roebuck the type of guy who would jump out of bed in the morning, excited to see if he could beat his sales volume record from yesterday? Not really. But his business partner was precisely that type of man. It was in his DNA to constantly learn how a new sales technique could up his closing rate by a few percentage points. Roebuck would've done well in life if he had never met Sears, but in this equation, the sum of the outcome far outpaced the individual parts. A team can accomplish much more than individuals. Sears was the "front office" and Roebuck was the "back office"—both were critical elements in a synergistic relationship. They expanded and grew the company.

Then a new concept appeared in the United States. It was named cash on delivery (COD). This system affected merchandise that was ordered through catalogs or other advertisements and paid for when the items reached their destination. You can imagine the reaction of customers: "What? I can order something from a catalog and pay for the item when the postal service delivers it to me? Never heard of such a thing!"

Sears realized that this new way of selling products could drive huge changes in American retail. This meant that a person living in Oklahoma could order a product from a company back east and not have to pay until it arrived on a train. The ease of transaction for the customer just became infinitely simpler. This program now required the U.S. Postal Service to collect the payment and return that revenue to the company. This was a game changer!

From there, Sears and Roebuck quickly exploited a new marketing avenue. It was just after this change in the retail industry that the Sears and Roebuck catalog became an American icon. The marketing brilliance of Mr. Sears allowed him to personally write a majority of the product descriptions contained in their massive catalog. Their catalog became so common that in some rural areas of the country, families only had two books within their household. One was the Bible, and the other was the Sears and Roebuck catalog. Each night by candlelight or in front of the fire after the family completed their day's work, they could study scripture and then indulge in reading about products from around the world. They could learn about products that they didn't even know existed.

These craftily written depictions were so enticing that Americans started ordering. It was fun to read, as it wasn't just a list of products. It was a book of dreams. Once the flamboyant description was read, you could not live one more minute without it. Possessing this item would complete your life's happiness. Through this new communication method, Sears had positioned their brand as aspirational—their products and brand identity made customers feel like they were achieving something by ordering, which is one of the strongest brand strategies used even today.

The company grew to an unbelievable magnitude. The catalog eventually started selling pre-manufactured houses in 447 different designs. Once ordered, the house would be delivered on a train and then assembled by the owner. And this all started with two entrepreneurs selling *pocket watches*!

The Sears and Roebuck fulfillment warehouse in Chicago was larger than 3 million square feet. At one point, they were receiving so many order forms by mail, they would occasionally lug wheelbarrows of unopened envelopes (orders) to the back of the property and burn them. Too many orders! Too many customers! All businesses have problems and issues, but if you ever start your own business, too many customers is *the* problem to have.

As the dilemma increased in size, Roebuck continually tried to strengthen supply chains and fulfillment. But when Sears (the neverending marketer) heard about this, legend says that he ordered 50,000 more catalogs. His theory was that a company with excessive demand will survive and grow.

That is the Sears and Roebuck story. A business can never have too many orders. I wanted to make sure my children understood this concept as they were contemplating their own businesses. It was also my goal to one day be a part of a company that emulated this story. Sears created an insatiable demand for his product. Just like today, the U.S. government seeks to create an insatiable demand for its number one product. To do that, a great salesman is needed, plus a never-ending fantastic marketing strategy.

As I've said, I am a good salesman, but I know I am not a *great* salesman. (Just like I know I am a good baseball pitcher but not a great one.) In all the businesses I have had over my lifetime, particularly in my most successful ventures, I was blessed with brilliant business partners who were much like Sears—partners who enjoy talking on the phone, attending charity functions, sitting on the board of directors for many foundations, and marketing endlessly from morning to night. I personally do not have that mindset, that natural desire. But some people do.

Sears always focused on the outcome. For the company he and Roebuck founded, too many customers solved a lot of other problems. And, to increase the probability of that kind of success, always have your opportunity antennae up. The Fed can never have too many customers for its number one product. Create insatiable demand, control competitors (like Bitcoin), and make the U.S. dollar the center of all global transactions.

Selling No-Solicitation

Great entrepreneurs are on continuous alert for new income ideas. Years ago, one of my teenage sons scuttled into the kitchen and gushed, "Dad . . . Dad I got this great business idea—you're going to love it! It's the perfect business model and fulfills a great need in the marketplace!" He was so excited—his eyes bright, a large smile illuminating his face as he explained this new business model.

Before I tell you about my son's great idea, we need to give a little background on how our family likes to operate. We have always put a premium on clever wit and a play on words—the ability to articulate two things at the same time using the exact wording. It's hilarious and great fun. (It also shows a glimpse of brilliance.)

What do I mean? You said, "Buy Bitcoin," to which I reply, "No, no, no . . . I said, 'Bye Bitcoin.'"

To illustrate further, years ago, Tesla fully electric cars were new to the market. I purchased a Tesla Model S, dark grey, with grey rims and dark black tinted windows. I was racing around in this incredibly fast car—showing off, blasting around corners, the whole deal. Seemingly out of nowhere, a police car appeared with its flashers bright in the rearview mirror. I pulled over, and an officer walked up to the driver's side. He was obviously admiring the car; it was probably the first electric car he had seen. I pushed the electric button to roll the window down. The officer leaned forward.

"Do you know why I pulled you over?"

Then I remembered what one of my business partners said to a police officer when he was pulled over in his Tesla model S. I paused, my face edging into a little smile, looked up at the officer and said: "Because I let you!"

The officer giggled and had to step back to compose himself. Needless to say, just like my business partner, I *didn't* receive a ticket. This is the genre of humor that my sons have grown up in. They had heard countless stories like this over the years.

Back to my son's business idea. The first thing he said was that this had to be a door-to-door sales model. We could not do this over the phone or use any other kind of sales or marketing technique.

In theory, we would have teams of people in each major American city go door-to-door on evenings and weekends selling this product.

The idea that my son was so excited about was selling "No solicitation" signs door-to-door. As I started to laugh, my son said, "No, wait, Dad, let me explain." As he outlined it, there would be three levels of signs, all of which would say "No solicitation":

- The first would be a paper sign that you place in your window.
- The second would be a plastic sign that you post outside your house.
- The third would be a metal sign that you could bolt to your door or the brick side of the house.

The sales pitch would also be really easy to teach. All the salesperson would say is:

- "This first sign keeps everyone off your porch for five dollars."
- "The second sign keeps everyone off your porch for ten dollars."
- "Check this out—twenty dollars keeps everyone off your porch."

I was laughing so hard, I had to go to the bathroom. As I walked down the hall, my teenage son followed, explaining why this was such a great idea. He kept talking as I shut the door. Through the door, he explained how to close the sale by reading the following script: "If there was ever a time in your life that you needed a 'No solicitation' sign, that time is right now, this minute. Just take out your wallet, and we can finish this perfectly timed transaction."

If the homeowner doesn't buy, the salesman would ask:

"Do you want me to come back tomorrow?" The perfect product for the perfect moment!

I came out of the bathroom laughing. His idea was dazzling. It fit perfectly, completely thought out, through every possible chess move on a hypothetical front porch. It was all-encompassing. He created a problem, and then he had the solution—not later, but right then and there. His product could solve an in-your-face problem with a $5 bill, a $10 bill, and of course the Holy Grail—a $20 bill.

With his entrepreneurial antennae extended, my son had found a fit—using humor and language that communicated multiple things within a few short sentences. I told my son that this reminded me of the actor Michael Keaton playing the character Billy Blaze in the movie *Night Shift*. As a business idea pops into his head, he says into a recorder: "Quick, phone StarKist and tell them to feed mayonnaise directly to the tuna." Ha!

> NOTE TO SELF
> ## Go After What's Missing
> Great leaders identify deficiencies and quickly fulfill each deficit, with talent other than their own, for complete perfection.

Finding things that fit together is the mindset of an entrepreneur. Constantly seeking two things that have apparent similarities is one attribute of a business mind. And sometimes even coincidental fits, or random and lucky unexpected, serendipitous outcomes can produce extraordinary results. Finding things that fit together is step one in business success. But having a mind that continues to search for things that fit together is a factory of business ideas—not just a one-shot deal.

Defeat the Terminator

One day an employee of mine, Sarah Connor, walked into my office and told me that she was going to be terminated in thirty days. I did not really know Sarah that well but asked her what she meant. She explained that her superior (the so-called "Terminator") was unhappy with her work and had put Sarah on thirty days' probation. He said that unless major improvement magically appeared, she would be terminated on day thirty.

That Thursday evening, we talked as other employees were clocking out and going home. Sarah worked in a division of the company administered by one of my other business partners. I explained that I did not understand her job description or the details of what was expected of her, but I did tell her that I was very good when it came to strategy.

We talked for more than an hour. At times during the conversation, her eyes watered with emotion. She did not really understand why she was on probation. She said that her boss (my business partner) just hammered into her over and over that "she just wasn't getting it." With a solemn face, Sarah exclaimed, "I don't know what *it* is. I don't know what the Terminator is talking about or what he really wants me to do."

The next hour was filled with questions—what *could* she do? I kept repeating to her that I didn't understand her job and therefore didn't know exactly what she needed to improve on. All I had to go on were two facts: (i) her job title was a real estate analyst, and (ii) she had thirty days to fix the problem. Neither of us knew exactly what the problem was; therefore, fixing it was akin to reading a mystery novel.

I decided to focus on the outcome rather than the methodology. I asked her to picture herself thirty days from now. It's a Saturday afternoon, and she is home watching TV on her couch. One of two scenarios is going to be relevant at that point.

First scenario: She will still be employed.

Second scenario: She will be unemployed.

I told her:

Imagine yourself on that Saturday afternoon looking into a mirror intensely, locked on your own eyes and saying to yourself: "I did everything I possibly could to keep that job." If that is true thirty days from now, then under both scenarios can you live with yourself?

That means during those thirty days, you maximized your efforts, you didn't leave one rock uncovered, and you didn't leave one report or task undone or completed shoddily. You did everything and anything that was in your power to possibly do—and, from there, tried to go even further. Sarah, if you can say these words to yourself thirty days from now, then that is all you can control. You did your very best.

What you don't want to do thirty days from now is look into the mirror and say: "You know, I should have worked that Thursday evening and gotten that report done early for Friday morning's meeting. Or I should have researched the data on this one property so that when my boss asked me for the average electric bills, I would have known that off the top of my head."

Sarah, you don't want to be that person who continually thinks: *I should have. I could have.* Sarah, don't be that person. That would be a very hard person to live with.

If you and your friends are planning to go snow skiing this Saturday, get on the phone and cancel it. Spend that time in the office becoming the best you can be. Earmark that time to research concrete prices in Texas, so if it comes up in a meeting next week, you won't have to look it up. You will know it in real time. On the very spot.

If you are going on a date with your boyfriend Kyle next Tuesday night, take a rain check. Use that time to fill out forms and reports for the tax assessments on the properties you analyze. Maybe you can save the company some money by finding a few more tax write-offs. Be here late, stay all day Saturday, and become an expert at your job. Imagine that your colleagues don't need to Google information. Instead, they come to your office and ask you. Because you know everything. Become Google in human form.

When your boss asks you what tax rates on our buildings in Texas are, you just rattle off those numbers at the Terminator so fast it sounds like an Uzi machine gun. You won't have to go and look them up or ask somebody else for information. You need to become "the expert." Nobody knows the property better than you. No one has the statistics that you have—revenue projections, prices of paint per gallon, maintenance costs, etc. You are the authority. Got a question about Texas properties? Sarah is the specialist to ask.

Sarah left my office that night discouraged but with a glimmer of hope. She had a strategy for possible success. But more importantly, she had a plan for self-integrity. Either way, however this whole thing worked out, she would be a better person. To my amazement, she did it. She put in the time. She worked late and on the weekends. She became an expert and satisfied the Terminator's resolve. Her career soared.

Some people would not have done it. Some people would not have risen to the challenge. But she started asking the right questions. She stopped asking what she currently was and started asking *What can I become? What are my possibilities? How can I find and fulfill my personal potential for excellence?*

Her efforts lifted her to levels of self-confidence previously unimaginable. From that point on, Sarah became indispensable to the Terminator. She was just too good. Smart business owners don't fire "too good."

Four years later, Sarah was back in my office, recounting the story of the pep talk I gave her that evening that helped her see the vision of who she could become—who she should become. It was a moment in time that changed her probability of success. Why was she in my office again? She had just received a major job offer from one of the largest real estate firms in the state. Her compensation package and new responsibilities were huge. I told her the company was going to miss her but congratulated her on the new position. She thanked me for what I had done for her. But I reminded Sarah that it was not me, as I only made a suggestion. A suggestion is the easy part. She was the one who actually followed through and improved her world. My suggestion would have been worth absolutely zero without her diligent effort and hard work.

Over the years I have used this same speech with my kids, their friends, and many other people who ask what they should do to improve their chances of success. Answer: invest in yourself.

Most people function better when they have a plan to succeed. Everyone needs a good strategy for success. There is never a guarantee of success. But it's not a guarantee of success that inspires people. It's the *chance*—or better said, the *probable outcome* of success—that lifts a person to new heights.

Selling Oranges vs. Skiing

The spark that lit my flaming desire to be my own boss and to be the one in control of my dreams happened when I was still in high school. Since camping sounded fun, I joined a Boy Scout troop one summer. A three-day hike through the mountains in a heavy rainstorm was challenging, but what I learned from the business side of my scouting experience was life-changing. Using our own skills and ideas, we were required to earn the money needed to pay for our varied activities.

At the time, another nearby scout troop had operated a successful fundraiser for several years. It involved going door-to-door for a few weeks selling cases of fresh oranges to be delivered at a later date. This was time-consuming—knocking on doors, getting orders, collecting money, and then delivering the product when it arrived. Still, it was good, honest work, enough that the troop earned about $600, which was enough to pay for their activities for an entire year.

NOTE TO SELF
Launch Your Great Idea into a Great Business Plan

The zenith of business plans was a private company (the Fed) obtaining the contract to create and promote the currency for the world's only super power. This is the most successful business plan in history. Study it and learn.

Our troop leader was a true businessman at heart. He was always seeking to accomplish his goals faster, better, and more efficiently. He focused on outcome—a genuine results-driven entrepreneur. He asked our troop if we wanted to sell oranges for a month. Or, he added, were there any better ideas?

When any entrepreneur seeks to start a business, one of the most effective formulas to use is OMR—that is Outcome, Method, Resources. This approach must be executed in that very order to achieve maximum results. As we've discussed, successful ventures focus on the desired outcome, first and foremost. To inspire greatness, you first need to define what you really want—to visualize the end, the conclusion.

Many people make the mistake of talking about their resources first instead of the outcome. For example, when people get together to do a fundraiser for a local charity, the first question they often ask is, "How much money do we have to work with?" That's a mistake. Starting with current resources inadvertently limits yourself and hinders possibilities. If someone says that you have $500 to launch a fundraiser for a local charity, most people will then go about designing a program that can facilitate a $500 budget—all because the charity committee decided to talk resources first rather than the outcome that they wanted.

By contrast, if the organizing committee discussed the outcome—defining specifically what they want to accomplish—then and only then would they be inspired to seek out methods to obtain that goal. Once the methods are defined, only then do you inventory the resources. For example, by first addressing the goal, then considering a budget of $500, even the most grandiose goal will already be etched into the minds and hearts of the committee. This makes even a tiny $500 budget a moving target as opposed to a hard fact.

Committee members will start to get creative rather than restricting their sense of possibilities. The bar is automatically placed higher, and people are focused on reaching it.

If the budget is not large enough for their vision, then committee members might think of a benefactor who could donate additional funds—driven by the outcome they wish to achieve. To do something outstanding, one must do OMR in the right order. All other formulas will generate less than optimal—less than possible—results.

Everyone has heard the saying "if you can dream it, you can achieve it." Build the dream with a solid vision. Then define your methods of execution—then and only then talk about existing resources. OMR in that specific order. This is how entrepreneurs accomplish what others can't imagine.

Back to my scout troop. Selling oranges sounded like a lot of boring work. We focused on the outcome and asked a simple question—Was there a way to have fun while fundraising at the same time?

Broken down into OMR:

> **Outcome:** We wanted to raise $600 and have a great time doing it.
> **Method:** Some type of party or event that people would pay money to attend.
> **Resources:** A troop member's father owned a large commercial bus that we could use.

Most people wouldn't view a bus as much of an asset, but to our business-minded troop leader, it was gold. We all lived in Las Vegas, Nevada—a location with very few snow skiing opportunities. The closest decent ski resort was located in Cedar City, Utah, which was about a four-and-a-half-hour drive. That made for a total round-trip drive time of nine hours, with only six hours of skiing. That promised an exhausting day, but we figured out a way to make it work. The troop decided to offer a ski package to the two area high schools. Sleep on the bus for four hours, ski all day, and sleep on the bus ride home, for a price of $30. We printed out flyers and posted them all over the two schools. We sold out in a week. Even better, we negotiated a group discount for the lift tickets.

The outcome: After all the expenses—fuel, lift tickets, etc.—our scout troop skied all day for free and also netted over $600.

This troop organized the same fundraiser for the following ten years after our initial idea. This single business experience gave me the confidence that one day I could be my own boss. My mind started to dream of all the businesses I could own and operate. For the first time in my life, I was able to experience the business side of a transaction as opposed to being a customer. And the kicker was, we had fun skiing while making money. It did not seem like work, because it really *wasn't* work.

> *"A person who loves what they do never works a day in their life."*
> —Author unknown—sometimes credited to Confucius

It now was crystal clear. I could sell oranges door-to-door or go skiing for a day. Easy choice!

OMR: focus on outcome, then methods, and then resources—in that order.

Selling Oranges vs. Skiing—on a Global Scale

China and Russia are executing their own version of going skiing rather than selling oranges door-to-door. But it seems as though the United States got on the slopes before they did. Those two countries are actively working to dethrone the U.S. dollar as the world's reserve currency. I don't blame them. If I were them, I would probably seek the same goal.

One method is to accumulate gold. The president of China just changed the country's constitution, which could enable him to be president for life. Notwithstanding the war in Ukraine, Vladimir Putin has been the president of Russia for twenty-plus years and is expected to be president for twenty more. From their perspective, the U.S. president is just a temporary employee—a figurehead at times, with a short four- to eight-year timeline. Russian and Chinese presidents have the luxury of long-term financial schemes. American presidents do not.

The U.S. dollar has a couple of wolves stalking in the shadows. Those wolves are China and Russia. Both are formidable individually, but they are a true threat as a team. The United States needs a junkyard dog–type campaign to protect its number one product. Washington, DC, is seeking to box in China and the yuan because they are threatening the dominance of the U.S. dollar on world oil transactions.

China and Russia may be wolves to the United States dollar. A real live wolf in the forest has pups of its own to feed. Therefore, I don't blame the wolf for trying to eat me. Nevertheless, I am determined to help the junkyard dog win. The wolf has a different set of objectives than I do. Like not getting eaten.

In 1960, 45 percent of the global currency reserves were held in U.S. dollars. By 2001, it had risen to 73 percent, and now it is about

58 percent of all the world's central bank reserves. With the Euro having 20 percent, Japanese yen at 6 percent, and the Chinese yuan at just under 3 percent. For comparison, the Canadian dollar has about 2 percent, and the Australian dollar also has about 2 percent. BRICS countries can try to trade in their own currencies, but they run the risk of accumulating paper assets that can decline much faster than the U.S. dollar will.

How does the U.S. dollar strengthen when inflation is also increasing? Think of it this way: The world wants green energy and starts investing in wind, solar, and electric cars. A lot of people stop investing in oil production and exploration. The result—less oil for everyone means higher-priced oil for everyone.

The world wants to move away from the U.S. dollar. Fewer countries invest in creating Eurodollars around the world, so the Fed shrinks the supply. The result—short supply equals higher priced U.S. dollars.

Simply, the world cannot move away from crude oil until it has a viable alternative to take its place. Therefore, oil prices will probably be high for years to come. The U.S. dollar has a similar basic supply-and-demand structure. It is difficult to replace the U.S. dollar until there is a viable alternative.

Over the last twenty-five years, China has had the greatest growth of any country in the history of the world. And over that time, the yuan has gone from 0.2 percent to 2.7 percent of all world currency reserves. On that trajectory, if China can continue growing at the same rate over the next twenty-five years, then would they overtake the Japanese yen at 6 percent of world currency reserves?

How far will the United States go to protect its number one product? China says they are going to stop using the U.S. dollar for oil transactions as they continually petition Saudi Arabia to accept the yuan as a transaction currency. The United States has countermoves. Make Saudi Arabia think twice about switching to the yuan. Using a classic Federal Reserve strategy, tell the public that we are trying for a 2 percent inflation rate but secretly seek an 8 percent inflation rate. Why? Increasing the interest rates on U.S. Treasuries from 1 percent to 5 percent strengthens demand for the dollar vs. China's yuan. This will enable the Saudis to purchase U.S. Treasuries at nearly 5 percent interest rates. At the same time the U.S. would remind them about the Nord Stream I and Nord Stream II pipelines—which were both destroyed by someone with a deep-water submarine.

High inflation rates will slow U.S. imports from China as American consumers worry about unemployment and a recession. Simultaneously, placing large tech sanctions on chips and materials sold to China will hinder its ability to produce products for world consumption.

This one-two-punch strategy weakens an already highly leveraged Chinese economy. China's unemployment will skyrocket, resulting in mortgage defaults. Forty percent of China's GDP is real estate, and collapsing that sector will cause economic strain on the entire country and the strength of the yuan. This results in printing more yuan—simultaneously weakening the currency and forcing China to print more currency than the U.S. does.

The United States will convince companies to pull out of China and start manufacturing elsewhere, concentrating commerce in regions of the world where the U.S. dollar is used for oil purchases. China's economy shrinks, and, they hope, over time the Chinese will realize that trading oil in U.S. dollars is a small price to pay for access to U.S. markets and investors. The U.S. strategy may not work, but China's economy will weaken alongside the diminishing strength of the yuan—thus boxing in China like the Fed boxed in Bitcoin.

The other result is that Saudi Arabia will be glad they did not switch to the yuan, and they will understand what the United States did to China and remember the Nord Stream pipelines. China has set itself up as a target of the Fed, as China has too many problems: (i) China prints more money than the United States, (ii) their population will decrease in size from 1.4 billion to 750 million within the next fifty years, (iii) they own trillions of U.S. dollars—therefore crushing the dollar will destroy a very large asset for them, (iv) unemployment is increasing due to the technology sanctions and companies moving to South Korea, Vietnam, and India, and (v) China has to battle the Fed—which as you can see is a huge problem.

The United States (working as a team) protects and promotes its number one product. The U.S. dollar is so far ahead that if the yuan is going to become the world's go-to currency, it's not going to happen for decades—if ever. China imports 80 percent of its oil. The United States has a surplus of energy. China is an importer of food. The United States is a surplus food producer.

One of the reasons China cannot currently invade Taiwan is that the U.S. Navy could easily cut off almost all oil deliveries to China, and 180 days later they would have no gasoline. China has an Achilles heel, and they know it. This is the reason they are building pipelines to Russian oil. Until those (non-ocean) delivery methods are online, their hopes of regaining Taiwan are close to nil.

The Fed banks do have long-term plans for the future of their number one product—the U.S. digital dollar. Similar to an American entrepreneur planning a lifetime of success by boxing in their businesses, they are boxing in their success probabilities. They're insulating their business models from failure by mitigating risk, through whatever means are possible. I was born into the U.S.

dollar system. I did not invent it, and it may be the largest Ponzi scheme ever. I am not trying to stop waves, just find one and ride it as long as possible.

Frugality Is Difficult for Americans

Even though Americans can enjoy the leverage of the dominance of the dollar, other obstacles remain. One is frugality. Self-imposed frugality is one of the elements needed to obtain wealth in the United States. If done properly, being frugal allows you to take risks when they're warranted.

If I had a first and second mortgage on my home and two car payments, I'd know that when a great business opportunity came—which I believed would eventually arrive—that debt would hinder me from aggressively pursuing that opportunity. Therefore, I would miss it. Massive personal debt can kill the entrepreneur. It saps optimism—not only from you but also from your spouse and other family members. It's pervasive.

Low personal debt enables staying power. Most battles in history have been won by attrition. If you have staying power, you can win. Low personal debt is an entrepreneur's war chest. Right before launching my first private equity investment fund, my wife, Jane, started and owned an online teeth-whitening business. For a few very crucial years, her efforts greatly supplemented our family's needs, enabling my business-venture war chest to stay strong. Together, we had fostered a lifestyle of almost zero debt. Without this early adoption in our marriage to live well beneath our means, my supersized business idea might never have become a reality. Many people who want to go for the entrepreneurial moon shot do not have staying power because—often due to excessive debt—they lack a war chest.

Why is this so difficult to do in the United States? Because no one wants to drive a rusty car with a dent in the door. That's too much to swallow when going to your high school reunion. Some are simply too concerned with appearances. Even if your house is almost paid for, with just a few more payments to go, the ease of swiping your credit card and taking your family to Hawaii for a vacation versus the local lake is just too enticing. And, with that, an entrepreneur trades future massive amounts of wealth for short-term status with friends and family.

I have a friend in her forties who, between her and her husband, makes about $400,000 per year. Still, they're worried that they will not have enough savings to retire on. I told her about another friend who was born in Nigeria, didn't speak English, moved to the United States with just a few thousand dollars, and now owns several businesses. This person accomplished this all in about ten years. I asked her, "If I told him that you could not save enough for retirement by making $400,000 per year, do you think he would laugh? Would he think I was joking?" She immediately got the point. Again, that essential question: *Compared to what?*

Hedge fund managers earn massive amounts of cash dividends for their work. Schoolteachers also receive massive amounts of dividends from students thanking them for changing their lives. High school coaches do not make massive amounts of money, but that is not the dividend that they were seeking. Over the years, their students thank them time and time again for the example they set and the changes in their lives—thanks to their care and instruction.

Their success goal was not wealth—their success goal was learning how to transfer valuable knowledge to a younger, less experienced generation. They succeeded in their goals . . . but it took effort. They had to learn how to become an effective teacher, an interesting public speaker, and a person sensitive to students who have difficulty learning. All of this required a focus on succeeding at their goal. And they probably had the following formula as they became their students' favorite teacher:

1. They lived in the United States.
2. They kept themselves mentally and physically healthy.
3. They got up every day seeking to improve their teaching skills.
4. They probably started early in life with an unwavering focus on becoming excellent at teaching.

This is a formula for success that can be modeled for any profession or goal. And it also works for wealth building. To remind you, as a teenager, I remember looking into the mirror at myself and saying the following words: "I am not afraid of being poor, and I am not afraid of being old. I am just afraid of being old and poor at the same time."

To help me avoid this fear becoming a reality, one of my strategies was to stay nimble in business by being frugal. Because a U.S. citizen can live a frugal life, not a poor life, and still make financial dreams come true. The longer you stay frugal, the better chance you have of becoming wealthy. Some statistics bear this out:

- In 2019, immigrant entrepreneurs made up 21.7 percent of all business owners in the United States, despite making up just over 13.6 percent of the population and 17.1 percent of the U.S. labor force.
- From 1996 to 2011, the rate of businesses founded by new immigrants grew 50 percent. During the same period,

businesses established by native-born Americans dropped 10 percent.

- Taking that up a notch, 44.2 percent of 2020 Fortune 500 firms had at least one founder who either immigrated to the United States or whose parents were immigrants.[*]

It's almost like immigrants were farming in a desert in their former country, and once they arrive in America, they really appreciate and know what to do with rich, dark, and fertile soil. To them, the opportunity is precious.

Sometimes it can be a harsh reality. As COVID-19 restrictions were being lifted and to increase the productivity of his company, Elon Musk, the CEO of Tesla, asked employees to return to the office or "pretend to work somewhere else."

Seeking to implement a four-day workweek is a luxury Americans believe they are entitled to. Here is a challenge: Find an immigrant and try to get them to limit themselves to a four-day workweek. They will laugh in your face. The following is a true story that my youngest son tells when he speaks to large groups and is trying to teach the concept of being frugal:

> I grew up in a normal-sized house. My dad drove a car with 200,000 miles on it. It was a normal life. I was in college and always wanted to run my own business. I started several ventures—building websites, online marketing, and a Mandarin Chinese tutoring company with several employees.

---

[*] New American Economy, "Entrepreneurship: Immigrants and the Fortune 500," accessed August 2023, https://www.newamericaneconomy.org/issues/entrepreneurship/#:~:text=44.2%20percent%3A%20Share%20of%202020,generated%20by%20those%20firms%2C%20FY2019.

My Dad grabbed me one day and said: "You're like a chicken running around with its head cut off. I have talked to one of my business partners, and he has agreed to meet with you to discuss your career."

So, I set the appointment and drove my car through this beautiful neighborhood until I arrived at this massive home that took up almost two-thirds of the cul-de-sac. I knocked on the front doors, expecting a butler to appear and chase me off the property. But then my dad's business partner answered the door and asked me into the enormous home with an indoor basketball court, a huge pool, and a 20-mile view off the back deck over the valley. It was truly a breathtaking vantage point. He also had expensive sports cars in the huge garage. We sat down in his front room on enormous white leather couches and started to talk about wealth building.

He said, "Let me tell you the secret of the rich. Rich people send their children off to an Ivy League school, then get them a job on Wall Street for ten years. Then those kids are groomed to start their own private equity fund. And the generational cycle starts again. And that is how I have everything that I have. Your dad and I started these private equity investment funds years ago, and that is our secret. You need to start your own investment fund."

I was all in. I was sold. I asked him if he would tutor me on private equity investment funds. Instead, he said that I should go and ask my dad, because my dad knew even more about funds than he did. I didn't believe this entirely. "Yes," I said, "but you are obviously way more successful than my dad. And I want the type of life you have. The pool, the cars, the indoor basketball court. So, I asked again, will be my mentor?"

He leaned over, and quietly said, "I am going to tell you a secret. Your dad and I make the exact same amount of money."

My jaw dropped. I sat quietly, glanced up at the ceiling in disbelief. Then I said, very abruptly: "I have to go." I got in my car and drove directly home. I walked in the house, slammed the door, and yelled at the top of my lungs:

"Daaaaaad!!!??? What is going on?" I demanded. "Last week we went out to eat at Chipotle, and you wouldn't even let me buy a large soda."*

> NOTE TO SELF
> ### Build a Battleship
> Frugality can be your financial battleship. Remember, it's a campaign, not a 40-yard dash. Outlasting adversaries is a necessity, and having a war chest might be the key to long-term success.

The point is, I had always lived well beneath my financial means. Large sodas and otherwise, my family was fine. We had a good home; everyone had a nice-enough automobile. It was a great life. I was just plowing all of my money back into more and more real estate investment funds with great income potential. My wealth kept growing in my quest to crush my fear of being old and poor at the same time.

Okay, maybe I had gotten a bit extreme. But now that my partner had let the (proverbial) cat out of the bag, I went and purchased two Tesla Model Ss. I kept one for myself and gave one to my father for his seventy-sixth birthday. My wife got a brand-new Land Rover, my kids received new cars, and my mom got a huge budget to travel the world in first-class

---

* Okay, the part about the soda is not true; my son just uses this example on stage as a metaphor. Poetic license.

fashion. My wife and I even purchased a new car for her parents. I thought I could have kept my wealth stealthy for another five or so years, but that's all in the history books now.

After all my ups and downs as an entrepreneur over the years, I knew if I ever got into massive personal debt, then I was slowly kissing my dream of owning a very successful business goodbye. To have staying power, to be able to take on risk, to shoot for the moon, I needed the confidence to take care of my family while I built a business. And when the opportunity came along to start my own private equity investment fund—with the chance of being very successful, a really good probability—I was ready to go without a paycheck for fourteen months. Then once that first fund was up and running (BLoC Fund I) we started a second fund (BLoC Fund II).

Fortunately, I was positioned to take on hard times again. The great recession hit the world in 2008, just as we launched our third fund. Once again, I had to go without a paycheck for almost ten months. Still, I was so excited—it was the best time in eighty years to be in real estate. I knew we were so well-positioned to take advantage of the economic downturn that it seemed like the future was transparent. I could see success even before it happened. The crystal ball had finally aligned with my business training, including the failures and successes. My frugal savings, the university degree in economics, and my personal staying power (my war chest) enabled me to risk it—not once, but twice.

My sons learned to become diligent, hard workers. My oldest son (John S. Pennington VI) purchased his own car in high school with his own money, paid for his college education, and funded his two-year church mission in a foreign country. Hard work and frugality could have been his middle name. That's a feat that none of his peers even attempted. He had figured out life with little financial assistance from his parents. He became his own self-made man! After he graduated from law school at Arizona State University, he launched an investment fund a few years later on his own—again, without my financial help. He became a very successful attorney in the focused field of private equity investment fund formation. He has recently started a second private equity fund in the renewable energy field, again without my financial backing. My youngest son (Bridger Pennington) has launched several private equity funds (without my financial backing) and also owns a business (Fund Launch) that teaches entrepreneurs how to launch their own private equity fund. Like I always tell people: the Penningtons are a FUN and FUND family. Ha.

When you began reading this chapter, you wanted to learn the truth of how to increase the probability of becoming successful. Now that you have the truth, are you going to use the formula laid out here? Will this be a good day or a bad day for you? By the way, 95 percent of the people who read this chapter will do nothing! Just make sure you are among the 5 percent that do. Then experience what happens next!

BOXING IN BASICS

11A. Remember Sears and Roebuck. Having too many customers is a problem you *want*. Think of ways to continually increase demand.

11B. Always extend your personal antennae to find the next great idea.

11C. Become the expert. No one fires the "expert."

11D. Work smart. Be creative when considering solutions. Go skiing and let someone else sell oranges.

11E. OMR in that order—Outcome, Method, Resources. Otherwise, you're only inadvertently limiting your potential.

11F. Frugality is a superpower. Living smart will position you to financially take on great opportunity when great opportunities appear.

11G. "I am not afraid of being poor, and I am not afraid of being old, I am just afraid of being old and poor at the same time."

CHAPTER 12
The Perfect Question

In December 1999, I made a goal to start my own private equity investment fund. The right question was a pure epiphany: "How *can* I become a private equity fund manager?" I continued to ask myself this question over and over and over. I knew, when prompted, my mind would find the best solutions for me.

This was a huge turning point in my life. Since then, I make it a point to never ask why I cannot do something—I always ask how I can accomplish something, as we discussed in chapter 9. This attitude re-alignment was the impetus that enabled me, five years later in 2004, to launch my first private equity fund—Bridge Loan Capital Fund I, Limited Partnership.

Fast forward to the year 2021. My partners and I owned a constellation of private equity funds that cascaded their capital down throughout the U.S. real estate market. As a co-founder of this family of private equity funds, I did everything in the first six years from traveling to locations around the country for due diligence on a real estate property to meeting with and pitching potential investors the next day. The company grew fast, and we hired specialized, expert personnel, with my responsibilities becoming more focused on the longevity and stability of the enterprise as opposed to day-to-day operations.

For better or worse, my entrepreneurial days were long gone. At my core, I love starting businesses from scratch—the excitement in the early years is really fun. But the company had grown, scaled, and expanded, and my personal tasks became administrative: (i) Chief Compliance Officer (CCO) and point of contact for all issues regarding the U.S. Securities and Exchange Commission (SEC), (ii) Deputy Chief Financial Officer (Deputy CFO) with signing authority on more than 1,200 bank accounts at nineteen different banks, (iii) Anti-Money Laundering Officer (AMLO) for all of our Cayman Island private equity feeder funds, (iv) member of the Board of Directors—secretary, (v) in charge of procurement of insurance to protect company officers and directors, and (vi) director of the company-wide written plan for disaster and recovery of firm operations and risk management teams (protecting thousands of employees in thirty-three states).

Paperwork, forms, reports, and audits; paperwork, forms, reports, and audits—day after day. "Fun" doesn't describe it. Vital, necessary, and essential would be more accurate. A large company has different obligatory requirements than a small one. Drafting complicated, extremely detailed reports and populating the data to an exhaustive level with excruciating clarity and submitting it on an absolute deadline was not the most entrepreneurial of assignments.

Creation and enforcement of policies and procedures designed to detect and mitigate violations in compliance with all SEC rules and regulations for thousands of employees is challenging. Large companies like this are usually Registered Investment Advisors (RIA) subject to SEC regulations and audits. Deciding to operate a company like this requires becoming well acquainted with strategies that allow private equity investments to thrive and survive under sometimes overbearing federal regulations.

It helps to know some history. Hopefully, one day you'll be in a position like mine where it's essential to understand the environment. As you'll recall from chapter 2, after the great 1929 stock market crash, the government stepped in and formed the SEC. Hoping to mitigate a similar crash in the future, the SEC was able to implement the Securities and Exchange Acts of 1933 and 1934, which dictated securities laws for the next century. These acts were implemented with the assistance of Joseph Kennedy, the first head of the SEC and also father of a future president—John F. Kennedy. Other amendments and acts were added over the years. But ninety years later, the original acts are still the bedrock foundation of U.S. securities law.

Why was Joseph Kennedy the first chief of the SEC? It's kind of like asking the fox to teach you how to keep other foxes out of the henhouse. Joseph Kennedy made a boatload of money in the crash of 1929. Accordingly, he seemed to know his way around financial issues. The U.S. government knew to hire the fox.

The acts of 1933 and 1934 were a momentous change in securities laws that regulated how companies could and could not be funded in the United States. They were designed to protect the small investor from unscrupulous capital raisers while mitigating conflicts of interest in the investment banking industry. The new laws were so restrictive that they virtually eliminated the ability of small companies to raise capital and investment dollars. To soften this, the SEC came up with exemptions to the acts of 1933 and 1934 that would allow small companies, if they followed the rules, to raise capital on a controlled basis.

Running and operating private equity investment is about setting expectations. If you tell your investors they're going to receive 4 percent and you make them 5 percent, you are the greatest guy in the world. But if you tell your investors they're going to make 10 percent, but you're only able to return 8 percent, you're a scoundrel who cannot be trusted. Running a fund is about managing expectations and keeping those expectations within parameters that are not merely possible but also *probable*. Let's take a closer look at some factors that impact whether a fund manager becomes a hero or a heel.

Summary of Act of 1933 and 1934 Exemptions

In 1933 and 1934, small company regulations—labeled the 504 exemption—allowed you to raise $1 million per investment per year. The 505 exemption allowed you to raise $5 million. The most common exemption was the 506, which allowed you to raise unlimited amounts of capital, with one major requirement. When using the 506 exemption, you could not use advertising or general solicitation to attract investors. The reason was a 506 exemption was a private offering, not an advertising campaign.

One thing most people don't know is that more capital is raised using a 506 exemption in the United States than all the money invested in the New York Stock Exchange and NASDAQ combined. That's because advertising is prohibited—or at least it *was*. In 2012, under the Obama administration, new legislation forced the SEC to split the 506 exemption into two major categories. Currently, the traditional exemption is a 506(b) exemption with no general solicitation; the new second category is a 506(c) exemption that allows advertising and general solicitation.

Major Differences between a 506(b) and a 506(c):

- A 506(b) cannot advertise for investors; a 506(c) can advertise for investors.
- A 506(b) can have as many as thirty-five non-accredited investors; a 506(c) must have 100 percent accredited investors. These are people with a certain high level of income—non-accredited investors don't have to meet these requirements.
- In a 506(b), investors can self-verify themselves as accredited investors. In a 506(c) the fund manager has the responsibility to verify each investor as accredited; self-verification is not allowed.
- If an investor in a 506(b) says they are an accredited investor and the fund manager is comfortable with that, then the fund manager's job regarding investor status is complete. In contrast, a 506(c) fund manager must obtain copies of investors' tax returns or letters from a licensed attorney, licensed CPA, or licensed investment advisor stating that their client is accredited. These types of third-party verifications are required before they can invest in the 506(c) fund.
- The most common filing is a Regulation D, Form D, 506(b), 3(c)1. This type of investment entity allows as many as 100 investors, thirty-five of whom may be non-accredited. This fund can raise unlimited amounts of capital but cannot advertise or use general solicitation. The second most common filling is Regulation D, Form D, 506(c), 3(c)1. Under this filing the entity is also allowed up to 100 investors, all of whom must be accredited investors verified

by a third party. This fund can also raise unlimited amounts of capital and, unlike 506(b) can employ advertising and general solicitation.

Quiz time! Which type of fund do you think the SEC watches most closely? Answer: The one that uses general solicitation and advertising to find investors. One reason has to do with the sorts of investors who can put their money into such funds. There are four main categories of individual investors.

1. **An Accredited Investor:**
   - Has a $1 million net worth, not including primary residence; or
   - Makes $200,000 a year; or
   - Makes $300,000 a year if a spouse's income is included; or
   - Is a general partner and in some specific cases a "Knowledgeable Employee" as defined by the SEC or holds FINRA's Series 7, 65, or 82.
2. **A Non-Accredited Investor** meets none of the requirements above.
3. **A Qualified Client** has a $2.2 million net worth, not including primary residence.
4. **A Qualified Purchaser** has $5 million of investments, not including primary residence.

Note: For most entities to be a Qualified Purchaser, they must have $25 million of investments.

The significance of this is a fund that only accepts investors considered Qualified Purchasers (Regulation D, Form D, 506(b),

3(c)7) is allowed 2,000 investor slots and is still considered a private offering. But, from the SEC's perspective, if more than 2,000 Qualified Purchasers have invested in the fund, by definition, this would violate the 1940 Exchange ACT and be defined as a "public company." Accordingly, the exemption under 506 would not be valid. Basically, the SEC does not believe that any one private company has 2,000 friends with over $5 million each of investments, not including their primary residence.

This is all a great deal to swallow and may seem unduly regulated. Still, the United States is one of the most fertile environments for entrepreneurs on the planet. And inside this very rich and abundant country, one of the best financial vehicles that can scale up a business idea or business model is a private equity fund/limited partnership, operated by a fund manager/general partner. That's because a limited partnership can accomplish things that individual investors struggle with. The economies of scale are indeed powerful. The next section illustrates that very point.

> NOTE TO SELF
> **Friends with Money**
>
> A supersized business requires financial friends. Create them by having deposits at multiple banks. Emulate the U.S., which cascades its currency throughout the planet, i.e. the G7, NATO, and the North American Trade Agreement.

How an 8 Percent Loan Can Yield an 18.62 Percent Profit

An investment fund can do things that an "average" wealthy person cannot. One such superpower is loaning money at 8 percent but returning a 18.62 percent profit. Here's how it can work with a large real estate loan for a very large organization such as Blackstone or BlackRock.

Scenario #1

A borrower wants to purchase a multi-state storage unit portfolio for $100 million. The borrower has $25 million in cash and needs to borrow $75 million at an 8 percent interest rate. A wealthy person lends the $75 million at 8 percent for twelve months, receiving $6,000,000 in interest payments. This lender could also charge a 1 percent loan origination fee of $750,000. Therefore, for the twelve-month loan, this wealthy person would receive 8 percent ($6,000,000) plus 1 percent ($750,000) for a total of $6,750,000 in profit.

That's far short of an 18.62 percent return.

	Provide a Loan at 8% Interest Rate and Make a 9% Yield			
	Borrower purchases a five-state portfolio of storage units at $100mm	$100,000,000		
	Borrower pays $25mm cash down payment	$25,000,000		
8%	You lend $75mm at 8% for a term of 12 months	$75,000,000	$6,000,000	1 year loan interest at 8%
1%	You charge 1% origination fee	$750,000	$750,000	1% loan origination fee
			$6,750,000	Total gross profit on loan
	$6.75mm divided into $75mm is a 9% return on investment	9% return		**9% is a long way from 18.62%?????**

That is correct! The loan only produces a 9 percent return—that's how an individual wealthy person would do it. What follows is how a large private equity fund such as Blackstone or BlackRock would structure the loan for an 18.62 percent return.

Scenario #2

The same lender specifics as the first scenario are in place— a multi-state storage unit portfolio, $100 million purchase price, $25 million cash down payment, and the need to borrow $75 million at an 8 percent interest rate. Like the wealthy individual, a fund would lend the $75 million at 8 percent for 12 months. But where does the private equity fund get the money to lend?

The fund would first "capital call" $20 million (this refers to collecting funds from private investors—the limited partners). Next, the fund would borrow the remaining $55 million from its favorite bank. This enables the fund to loan $75 million to the borrower. The $20 million from investors would earn 8 percent in interest for one year—$1,600,000.

Additionally, as the fund borrowed $55 million from the bank at 5.5 percent and then loaned it at 8 percent, it earns a profit spread of 2.5 percent on $55 million—$1,375,000. Like the individual lender, the fund charges a 1 percent loan origination fee of $750,000. Total revenue; $1,600,000 + $1,375,000 + $750,000 = $3,725,000. Divide that into the $20 million the fund put in from its investors—an 18.62 percent return. That is how a large private equity fund produces an 18.62 percent rate of return by making a 8 percent interest rate mortgage loan. They leverage investor capital.

	Provide a Loan at 8% Interest Rate and Make a 18.62% Yield			
	Borrower purchases a five-state portfolio of storage units at $100mm	$100,000,000		
	Borrower pays $25mm cash down payment	$25,000,000		
	Where did the $75mm come from?	$75,000,000		1 year loan interest at 8%
8%	Fund put in $20 mm from investors	$20,000,000	$1,600,000	Fund profit on the $20mm at a 8% interest rate
	Fund borrowed $55mm from the Bank at 5.5% interest rate	$55,000,000	$1,375,000	Spread profit between borrowing at 5.5% and lending it at 8%
			$750,000	1% loan origination fee
	$3,725,000 divided into $20mm is a 18.62% Yield		$3,725,000	Total Fund Profit = 18.62% IRR (internal rate of return)

Here, many people would be ready to ask several questions: Why would a bank lend a private equity fund $55 million, enabling the fund to then re-lend the money out to another borrower? Aren't banks in the business of lending *directly* to a borrower? The bank has many reasons to lend this money to the fund:

- The fund is a longstanding customer, and the bank values its continued business.
- Other banks would welcome the chance to grab a loan from a competitor.

- The bank isn't completely left high and dry. Since it borrowed the money from the Fed at 5 percent and loaned it out at 5.5 percent, it makes a 0.5 percent profit— $275,000.

But what about potential problems? Isn't a 75 percent loan to value a risky loan for the bank? Not at all. This is actually an extremely low-risk loan from the bank's perspective. For the bank to lose money:

1. The borrower would have to walk away from their $25 million cash down payment.
2. The fund would have to walk away from its $20 million cash equity of investor capital.
3. The fund would risk compromising its reputation with a well-established bank—not to mention every other bank.

Additionally:

1. If the borrower defaulted, the fund would love to own this property at a cost of $75 million. It would just buy out the bank's position.
2. The lending bank keeps other banks away and retains the large fund as a big cash depositor.
3. The bank's loan to value is only 55 percent, with two parties (the borrower and the fund) guaranteeing that the bank will not lose money.

It's a veritable slam dunk for the bank. It makes for a very safe loan and keeps a very large customer happy, retaining its business for years to come. The large scale of the business matters. This allows private equity investment funds to maneuver on a different level from a wealthy individual. A fund can provide its investors a larger return with basically the same risk. It's a matter of scale. They are large, and they use their volume and power to push banks to places that an individual simply cannot go. Large customers can make demands.

Similarly, the United States has been a large world partner of Saudi Arabia. Accordingly, they have used their influence to mandate that Saudi Arabia only sell oil in U.S. dollars. Why did the Biden administration cancel the Keystone Pipeline? On the surface, it doesn't make sense, unless we factor in that the United States must support world oil prices for the Saudis. Helping to suppress oil production worldwide is one more leverage point to convince the Saudis that continued sales in only U.S.-denominated dollars is a prudent business strategy. Again, large customers can make large demands on their banks. The strategy? Make it very painful for any country that ditches the U.S. dollar.

> **NOTE TO SELF**
> ### Size Matters
> To become large you need to scale, to scale you need to raise capital, and the easiest way to raise large amounts of capital is through a private equity fund structure. Size matters—the Fed taught me that!

Negotiate Like the Chief of Police

Let's revisit the issue of negotiation. As I've discussed, many people do not understand what negotiation is all about.

In war, trading one of our prisoners for one of your prisoners may on the surface seem like a good deal. Wrong! Negotiation is not about finding a perceived "fair deal." A good negotiator's job is to discover what the other party will or will not trade. A good negotiator might trade one of our prisoners for one of their prisoners plus a spouse and one child. And if a good negotiator discovers that this is what the opposing side is willing to trade, he's done his job as well as learned how far the opposite party will go—valuable knowledge for the future. It is not about a one-for-one trade. A ten-year-old kid can do that. Using many avenues and strategies, a savvy negotiator finds out what the opposing side will pay. That's the real job.

When a great negotiator is in the thick of it, they will encounter opposition from all sides. That's because 99 percent of the population does not understand what negotiation is. If a man is sent to negotiate a prisoner swap, his government, his boss, his wife, and even his children may get mad at him when they learn he is on the verge of killing the whole trade by trying to obtain two for one. They'll pester him not to push so hard, reminding him one for one is a perfectly fair deal.

But the negotiator's real assignment is usually lost amid the intensity and anxiety of the moment. Therefore, the negotiator has to manage all the anger and threats from his own boss, his own government, and even his own family, let alone those from the opposition. He is alone—an army of one. He has to face combat on all sides, even from his allies.

The only way a negotiator can survive and succeed is to completely and absolutely take charge. The buck stops with him. He must tell his boss or government that he's the negotiator, and they cannot tell him what to do. They can fire him but cannot tell him how to do his job. Lacking this attitude, the negotiator is hindered. He cannot truly find out what the other party's maximum pain threshold is, or phrased differently, maximum payment or maximum trade.

Here is a quick example of a police chief in any small town in America: There is a murder in the town, and the chief is investigating several suspects, one of whom is a very prominent citizen. The department is spending a lot of money and resources on this one particular suspect. Concerned, the city council calls a big meeting and confronts the chief. They tell him he's wasting his time and city funds investigating this very prominent citizen (although it's common knowledge the city fathers are far more worried about angering an important member of the community). Following a long and very combative discussion, one council member demands that the chief explain himself to the city council—who have the power to dismiss him.

> **NOTE TO SELF**
> ## Prepare to Negotiate
> Great negotiators practice in the mirror, run mock simulations with friends. They do not wing it; they are good because of practice, practice, and practice.

That's when the tough negotiator in the chief comes out. "Yes, you can fire me," he declares in response, "but you cannot tell me what to do. I am the chief of police; I have received a budget from the city council to administer as I see fit. I am the sole person responsible for that budget, with my sole discretion. I am currently within that budget; therefore, you have no grounds to fire me. But nevertheless, you can still fire me anytime. But, again, you cannot tell me what to do, because the buck stops with me—that is, until you fire me. You can give me advice, which I appreciate, but you cannot tell me what to do."

This is a negotiation move on the part of the chief. He is testing what the city council members are willing to do, willing to pay, to protect this very important citizen under investigation. The chief of police is negotiating from a very strong position. He's "setting the bit," as a horse trainer would say. This same attitude is held by successful presidents of corporations, by general partners and private equity fund managers, and by savvy chief compliance officers. When negotiating, you should adopt this very same mindset.

Compliance Is All In

It's true that you can negotiate a great many things. But compliance isn't one of them—a particularly important consideration for a growing investment concern. Still, effective negotiation can come in handy when it comes to compliance. Here's what I mean:

Once an investment company reaches $100 million RAUM (Regulatory Assets Under Management), SEC rules require that the entity become a Registered Investment Advisor (RIA). That makes it subject to the SEC's oversight and regulation. Additionally, all RIAs must have a designated chief compliance officer on file with the SEC. This person is responsible for making sure personnel in the company, and the company itself, comply with all SEC rules and regulations.

I seemed like the logical choice for our company. Previously, I had been a manager of a securities broker/dealer. Moreover, for the past several years I had taken responsibility for filing all our REG D, Form D submissions with the SEC. Even though my credentials suggested it, I became chief compliance officer (CCO) in a rather unusual way. My business partners unanimously named me to the position when I was away on summer vacation with my family. When I returned to work, I discovered my brand-new assignment. What a welcome back! I felt like they had just given me blueprints to build a navy aircraft carrier and were asking how soon can we set sail. "Overwhelmed" describes my emotions in that moment.

The reaction fit the moment. Every few years, using either an audit or examination, the SEC investigates company compliance to gauge how well that firm is playing by the rules. Usually, if a company is growing fast—meaning their RAUM is rising exponentially—the SEC will examine or audit that firm about every three to four years. These in-depth procedures can last four to six months on average and require enormous effort from the firm's staff.

I have never heard of an RIA (with a very large RAUM) receiving a 100 percent perfect score on their SEC exam. Still, it's worth going after. Even an almost perfect score on an SEC exam can be very attractive to potential investors. It bolsters credibility. A CCO who adopts the "police chief" negotiation approach that I described earlier gives the company the best chance at the best exam results possible.

No CCO receives great SEC exam results unless all partners and employees are extremely diligent and committed to a team effort. It is not easy to do—it takes determination from the entire team. But the buck truly stops with the CCO. And a realistic CCO understands that risk can never be completely eliminated. The moment you start a new business is the moment you take on risk.

That's why diligent CCOs develop a living document called a *risk matrix*. This involves running numerous probable scenarios, playing out in exaggerated ways what could happen under certain situations. And sometimes those scenarios suggest frightening outcomes—consequences that can demand bold steps to prevent.

Fun with Funds

Most private equity funds are organized under the entity of a "limited partnership" (LP)— not to be confused with a "limited liability company" (LLC) or a corporation (INC). An LP has over a hundred years of history, particularly in the state of Delaware. Some people try to use the LLC structure to do the same things that an LP is designed to do. You can structure an LLC just like an LP, but why would you go through the headache of reinventing the wheel? A good mechanic can take two Ford F150 truck engines and attach both to an airplane wing, and the plane will fly. But why would you do it?

Steve Jobs, co-founder of Apple, took his company public as a corporation. Stephen Schwarzman, co-founder of Blackstone, took his company public with the basic structure of a limited partnership. What's the difference? With a corporation, shareholders annually vote on who will run the company. As a result, Jobs was eventually bounced out of the iconic company he co-founded—one day president, the next day not. In contrast, Schwarzman is essentially the general partner of a limited partnership. Unless he commits fraud, the limited partners cannot get rid of him.

By definition, all limited partnerships must have a general partner (GP). That's why I decided in 1999 to become a general partner of my own limited partnership instead of a managing member of an LLC or a president of a corporation. My business partners and I didn't want to suffer Jobs's fate—building a great company only to be tossed out.

A limited partnership is akin to a pool of investor capital that has been entrusted to the general partner to invest in an area in which he or she has expertise. For instance, if you are an expert in medical office real estate, then you could be the general partner of a medical office real estate fund. An advantage with LPs is that they are aligned with the general partner's interests. If the fund's investments do well, the limited partners receive a great return on their capital and the general partner is also well compensated. The standard structure in real estate is known as a "two and twenty" (2 and 20). This means the fund pays a 2 percent annual management fee to the general partner or registered investment advisor. Additionally, the general partner receives 20 percent of all investment profits while the limited partner receives the remaining 80 percent.

But there's more. A good general partner will usually implement a "preferred rate of return." This is a more desirable payout. For instance, if the preferred rate of return is 8 percent, when a medical property is sold at a 20 percent return, the limited partners receive 16 percent, with the general partner pocketing 4 percent. But what if the investment only made 8 percent that year? Due to the preferred rate of return of 8 percent, the limited partners get 8 percent, and the GP receives nothing. If the investment made 8.5 percent, then the limited partners receive 8 percent, and the general partner only receives only .5 percent. But the GP isn't always on the short end. The "pref" or preferred rate of return has a waterfall. Once the 8 percent "bucket" is full (8 percent to the LPs), then any profit above that preferred rate of return is shared with the GP.

Be Grateful for What You Have

To an outsider, this fee structure may seem unfair. For instance, stockbrokers usually charge 1 to 4 percent; real estate agents charge 3 to 6 percent; but a general partner receives 20 percent of the profits, plus a 2 percent annual management fee. Unfair or not, that's the way things are structured. So, in 1999, when I learned that GPs make a hefty 20 percent, I knew I had to find a surfboard and ride that wave. Trying to stop the wave would only be futile. I decided to become an expert surfer on that specific wave. Consistent excellence always attracts talent and investors.

Still, as Confucius pointed out, "A journey of a thousand miles begins with a single step." What can I do to succeed? What would be my first step? Then, I remembered another quote, this one unattributed: "The secret to happiness is being thankful for what you have."

If you live in a slum and are thankful for what you have, you are happy. If you live in a mansion and are not thankful, it's hard to be happy. It's important to consider what you truly have. Are you happy with what you have? What will you do with what you have once you obtain it?

Very few companies in history have been able to accomplish all three of the following simultaneously, (i) INVESTORS receive a high and constant dividend, (ii) CUSTOMERS always want more of their product, and (iii) PERSONNEL rarely leave—attrition is low.

Tesla's customers are loyal, and employees love the products they produce, but investors do not receive dividends (two out of three—not bad).

Let's do an OMR.

"O" = **Outcome:** I wanted a supersized business that did three things simultaneously: (i) investors receive fantastic returns (dividends) on their investments; (ii) patrons have insatiable demand for our product; and (iii) employees are aggressively competing to be hired due to the reputation and company's industry lead.

"M" = **Methods:** (i) Utilize the private-fund structure to attract fantastically talented people using equity as an alignment of interests; (ii) utilize the private-fund structure to provide an alignment of interests for investors; (iii) utilize large quantities of investor capital to negotiate from strength; and (iv) provide transparency to investors, patrons, and employees.

"R" = **Resources:** The secret and competitive advantage of a private-equity fund structure is that **resources are not finite**. All businesses have problems, but the best problem to have is too many customers. The mantra of Mr. Sears solves most all other problems, meaning capital raising from potential investors never ceases.

Okay, I know what you're thinking, *John, John, John . . . how in the heavens can I learn to do all of this?*

The answer is simple—become a student of the number one product of all time. Study how its team members (the Fed, IRS, SEC, the president, and the U.S. Navy) seek to protect and promote with a goal of boxing in and controlling all competition. Use size, negotiation from strength, and never-ending marketing and distribution campaigns, all the while never forgetting about the legal system, written agreements, and not fighting waves of economic opportunities. Then do your best to duplicate all of it. Learn from the best. Study the GOAT.

1. **INVESTORS:** U.S. citizens enjoy the dividend and luxury of the world's reserve currency.
2. **CUSTOMERS:** The planet has an insatiable demand for U.S. dollars. It sells like hotcakes.
3. **PERSONNEL:** Ninety-nine percent of all U.S. citizens prefer living in the U.S.A. vs. other countries.

All three groups simultaneously fulfilled vs. alternatives on the planet. We all agree it is nowhere near perfection. Not even close. But compared to what?

Change yourself by changing the questions you ask. That relates to the core issues of this book. Private equity investment funds can make a tremendous impact for good. They just need good, honest, hardworking, positive people to run them.

It's Even Simpler than That

I started this chapter by discussing the right and wrong question to ask myself—what can I do, rather than why can't I do it. I think it is even simpler than that. When I was younger, I was continually taking small quizzes to discover who I was or what I was like. These little exams would then categorize me and my friends into a color, a number, or some animal, such as a lion or a hawk. But all this effort to find out who I was proved somewhat futile. Yes, it is nice to know who I am and what capacities I have or don't have. But asking myself over and over what am I, where do I come from, or who I am is not really the best strategy. They are good questions, but the real underlying question that I truly—and I mean truly— want to know is *Who can I become?*

Asking *Who am I?* may hurt a little when the answer cuts to the bone. *You are selfish. You are poor. You are a bad student.* Wow, that stings. I received the answer to the question I asked. However, the question I really want to know the answer to is: *How can I become smart? How can I become wealthy? How can I become charitable?* When I receive answers to these questions, I have a new life map to follow. They highlight possibilities rather than the present moment. The present can always be changed.

What I can become is the question that pushes me every morning. What is possible and probable? If you currently have a job washing dishes at a fast-food restaurant (as I did when I was in high school), then can you one day manage billions of dollars for investors? What can you do? Continually asking what you can become should be the zenith of your daily existence.

Asking this question repeatedly broadens your personal horizon. This is the question that I hope you start asking yourself every morning, every day, and every night. Even if this is the only habit or takeaway you glean from this book, it might just be the catalyst that delivers you to a destination ten years from now that may seem impossible at the moment.

As Bill Gates observed, "Most people overestimate what they can do in one year but underestimate what they can accomplish in ten years." One plus two always equals three. And, to reiterate, those three are:

1. Stay healthy.
2. Wake up every day and try.
3. Eventually you will succeed in the United States of America.

Don't expect overnight success. Some nights you will go to bed crying on your big pillow because you failed. Doesn't matter—wake up in the morning and try again. As Albert Einstein said, "In the middle of difficulty, lies opportunity."

A fund is complex—complying with SEC rules, managing investor expectations, keeping your team focused, problem-solving to deploy capital, improving assets, internal audits, fund administration, quarterly investor reports, raising equity capital, finding debt investors, finding accredited investors (or even better, Qualified Purchasers), deciding to have a fund which can advertise or not . . . and on and on it goes. Complexity continually fights reliability, but they can coexist. And a great team, brilliant partners, and dedicated, smart employees can make it happen—not just possibly but with a high degree of probability.

And if you can dream BIG, then becoming a general partner or fund manager of your own limited partnership or fund is an attainable goal.

You do not need to get an Ivy League degree (although it would help), and you do not need to work on Wall Street for ten years (although it would help). You just need to focus on what you can become rather than what you currently are. I started selling used blue jeans and ended up managing billions of dollars with an IPO on the NYSE. Blue jeans to billions. I got rich quick; it only took one billion seconds.

Where Should We Focus?

An old African proverb says: "If you want to go fast, go alone. If you want to go far, go together." Having learned to ask the right question—*How can I?* versus *Why can't I?*—I eventually learned to perfect the question by changing just one word. That word became my focus for the next decade and a catalyst of greatness.

It was the word *we.*

Scan the QR code to watch the author reveal how he
got rich quick—in only one billion seconds.

In 2008 the question changed to, *What **can we** become?* This small adjustment to the question was the magic ingredient that united the enterprise. More followed: *How far can **we** go? How can **we** become the best investment fund in the nation? How can we become the best team?*

Armed with these types of questions, your team, your company, and your enterprise could find itself twenty years from now managing billions of dollars. Without a really great team all rowing the boat in the same direction, the probability of falling short is very real. But align the interests of a great team, then train, practice, execute as a united front, as a combined force . . . and success is not only possible but probable.

What keeps me up at night?

Question to Self: If electricity ceased to exist, do I have any money? Hmmmm?

Final Note

Most people only read parts of a book. Thank you for finishing this book completely. Getting it done, done, done. Like that African proverb points out, "Together, we can go far."

Sincerely, your friend and econ geek,

John S. Pennington Jr.
JOHNSPENNINGTONJR.COM

Acknowledgments

Success in business sometimes attracts requests for advice. The assumption that wealthy people have a crystal ball and can predict your personal business future is erroneous. I don't believe in predictions, but I do believe in *probabilities*. The idea for this book was derived from the many mentoring discussions with my college-aged sons, nephews, and their friends. Entrepreneurs who are just starting out in life sometimes see gray hair as a possible source for business advice. As I focused on their goals, my lifetime of starting businesses with the dream of being my own boss enabled me to assist them in possible business maneuvers that have high probabilities of success.

My family regularly discusses the successes and challenges of all my entrepreneurial experiences. We do this with blunt honesty of the failures as well as successes. For these reasons, I was inspired to scribble down a book about business for posterity. Hopefully they will be able to glean some of my information based on years of experience. But more importantly, if my time on this planet ended early, I wanted my children to understand how I use strategy to avoid as many failures as possible. I improved my probabilities of success even with my disadvantages in life. I expect that most people long to leave a legacy of some kind; a remnant of having lived earnestly and offering a glimpse of their own unique personality to future generations.

I am blessed that my parents are (as of this writing) alive—and sadly, my grandparents are deceased. How I would love to hear their voices again, to remind me of their characters and their knowledge of how they overcame challenges. My hope is that this book will permit my children and grandchildren to hear my voice, catch a twinkle of my personality, enjoy my humor, and appreciate my dedication to their success. A transfer of knowledge, or even better—an exercise in deductive reasoning. A teaching model backed by experiences and hypotheticals. Something that I wished I had received when I was just starting out.

I am no business expert by any means. I just enjoy exploring and talking economics, business, and strategy. My thoughts and conclusions do not represent any investment advice or legal advice, and I reserve the right to change my opinion or my thoughts at any time in the future. (You should too, by the way!) The lure of being a published author seems glamorous and important—a worthy dream and goal. However, the difference between the spoken and written words is mystifying; making that transition took much more effort than I expected. Anyone can write a book, but can you write a book that people want to read? The challenge of succinctly wrangling off-the-hip original scripts with an understandable stream-of-consciousness into a readable manuscript is not easy. Therefore, I must give thanks to Jeff Wuorio for helping me make this a book people will want to—and will—read.

My wife, Jane, is a remarkable mother and the love of my life. I want to be a husband of whom she can be proud. The book you hold in your hands was inspired by our sons but is dedicated to the mother who carried them.

About the Author

JOHN S. PENNINGTON JR., in 2008, co-founded a family of investment funds that by the time of his retirement in 2021 was managing over $28 billion. During his tenure and before obtaining partner emeritus status, he served on the board of directors, held signing authority on over 1,200 bank accounts as the deputy chief financial officer, was president of over 100 corporations, was the anti-money-laundering officer for all of the company's Cayman Island feeder funds, and oversaw all U.S. Securities and Exchange Commission regulatory requirements as chief compliance officer. The company is listed on the NYSE and in 2022 was ranked thirteenth among the top 200 private real estate firms by Private Equity Real Estate (PERE).

In 2004 and 2007 he co-founded Bridge Loan Capital Funds I and II. In 1989 he co-founded an export company and served as its president for over 10 years. He attended Brigham Young University and then the University of Utah, earning an economics degree in 1988. John and his wife, Jane, were married in 1985 and have three sons and five grandchildren.

JOHN STEPHEN PENNINGTON VI (CONTRIBUTOR) is the co-founder of Doomsday Partners, a firm focused on sustainable renewable energy solutions and positive environmental impact. He is a seasoned transactional attorney and is licensed to practice law in multiple states. He formerly served as a partner at Kirkland & Ellis, one of the world's most prestigious law firms, facilitating capital raises ranging from $100 million to $6.5 billion. He has also served as chief compliance officer at Sundance Bay, a private equity firm exceeding $700 million in investments. John the VI holds a juris doctor degree from Arizona State University's Sandra Day O'Connor College of Law and a Bachelor of Arts degree from Brigham Young University. John VI and his wife, Kayla, have four wonderful children, all of whom are active in their local community.

BRIDGER O. PENNINGTON (CONTRIBUTOR) is the co-founder of Fund Launch, a company that has been instrumental in helping launch over 130 private equity funds, including eleven that each have over $100 million in assets under management. He is a co-founder and managing director of his own hedge fund. Prior to this, he was the founder and sole owner of two successful private equity debt funds. He is a sought-after public speaker and has been featured as a keynote at multiple live events, including crowds of over 2,500 participants. Bridger and his wife, Lauren, have one beautiful son and are active philanthropists.